2013
MAYAN
SUNRISE

2013

MAYAN

SUNRISE

Your Guide to Spiritual Awakening *Beyond 2012*

Wisdom Teacher Sri Ram Kaa
and
Angelic Oracle Kira Raa

Ulysses Press

Published by:
ULYSSES PRESS
P.O. Box 3440
Berkeley, CA 94703
www.ulyssespress.com

ISBN13: 978-1-56975-783-3
Library of Congress Control Number: 2009940337

Printed in the United States by Bang Printing

10 9 8 7 6 5 4 3 2 1

Acquisitions Editor: Kelly Reed
Managing Editor: Claire Chun
Editor: Richard Harris
Proofreader: Lauren Harrison
Production: Judith Metzener
Front cover design: DiAnna VanEycke
Cover images: pyramid © istockphoto.com / mammuth;
    light rays © istockphoto.com / joecicak
Interior images: page 22 © Shutterstock.com / Hannah Gleghorn; page
    35 Central America © Shutterstock.com / adam.golabek, Guatemala
    © Shutterstock.com / AridOcean; page 175 © Shutterstock.com /
    Vania Georgieva; page 195 hands © Shutterstock.com / Mudassar
    Ahmed Dar, globe © Shutterstock.com / Filipp Obada, lotus
    © Shutterstock.com / Anna Rassadnikova; page 201 ©
    Shutterstock.com / Danomyte

Distributed by Publishers Group West

contents

WHAT PEOPLE ARE SAYING ABOUT SRI RAM KAA AND KIRA RAA

"I feel a sense of joy when I am in touch with Sri and Kira. I feel like I am joining my essence with theirs and it feels wonderful!"

BARBARA MARX-HUBBARD, AUTHOR, SOCIAL INNOVATOR, AND PRESIDENT OF THE FOUNDATION FOR CONSCIOUS EVOLUTION

"...Two of the best examples of open-mindedness!"

— GEORGE NOORY, RADIO HOST, COAST TO COAST AM

"Sri and Kira inspire us to align our lives with our own authentic knowledge and discover that we are indeed divine co-creators. Transcending religion, Sri and Kira's message reminds us that our souls' wisdom is accessible."

WILLIAM J. BIRNES, STAR OF HISTORY CHANNEL'S UFO HUNTERS, MILLION-COPY SELLING AUTHOR, AND ACCLAIMED VISIONARY

ACKNOWLEDGMENTS

This amazing journey is a compilation of several years of intense travels, meetings, workshops, articles, and endless personal interactions with the Maya.

We give gratitude and thanks to all the amazing people who have contributed to this book coming to form. Without you, this gift of love would not be here, and each day we unwrap the gift of your love toward us!

The universe is expanding infinitely as our love and appreciation is extended to Carla, Ganeshananda, Jennifer, Janardan, Tranaii'ah, Michael, Ralph, the Ulysses Press staff, and the entire village of San Antonio Palopó. Thank you for your belief in this project and for your loving efforts to make this reality.

Our heart is fully present with the many Maya who have patiently laughed as we have tried to learn Cachikquel, and for their trust in us and acknowledgment of the sacred healing energies of TOSA La Laguna Self-Ascension Center in Guatemala.

Beloved Creator, hear us and feel our heart. We thank thee for the gifts bestowed upon all at this very moment and for the gift of bringing this book to form. We are infinitely grateful.

Many blessings of love,
Sri and Kira

FOREWORD

by Ronald James

It has been a long time since I first saw Sri Ram Kaa and Kira Raa on a stage in Sedona, offering an audience a chance to evolve and connect with deeper parts of their own selves. I remember they said, "If you feel compelled, come talk to us, we'd love to meet you."

My reaction to that was that it wasn't the usual hard sell. In fact, it was more of an invitation on a level of intuition, an energetic offering to a deeper level of the being. Now, years later, I have had the privilege of assisting Sri and Kira in the development of many videos, DVDs and presentations, as well as producing media for their live 2012 Events. The couple that I have come to know during this time have earned my utmost respect and trust.

I have sat quietly watching as Sri Ram Kaa ponders a conversation, takes a deep long breath, and slowly says something so profound that it resonates with me for days. I have watched the two of them play off of each other in candid conversations, as though the stream of words is coming from two mouths, yet only one soul. And with these two, after a while, that is not hard to imagine. I have come to know Kira Raa as a beautiful human being who worked incredibly hard through all of the mistakes we as people make, to arrive at a wonderful point in her most magical life.

Humanity seems to have this deep preoccupation with seeing people fall, for seeing them expose themselves as hypocrites, charlatans or worse. We watch our leaders, our advisors, our heroes with controlled skepticism, expecting the other shoe to drop. We revel in strange fascination as lives are deconstructed in the media, and as yet another great human being falls from grace.

I have seen Sri and Kira in many surroundings and situations. Behind the scenes in a chaotic event, deluged by people needing an endless supply of hugs, privately in their home and publicly while people questioned their motives, I have never seen them vary from being the people whose self portrait they paint across the planet. Like all of the great teachers, they honestly lead by example.

They are talking about a new level of humanity. A new paradigm of philosophy, mindset, interaction and power. We seem overwhelmed today by a media that delivers a steady stream of negativity, bloodshed, violence and a guttural state of being that we are told is our nature.

We watch the story unfold and may even have resigned ourselves to an unavoidable outcome of doom for our civilization. But for many of us, most of us, I believe, something isn't ringing true. Something isn't right. There's something we're not being told, but we feel it. And that is *exactly* why you should be reading this book.

Sri and Kira are here to reassure us that we don't have to drink the Kool-Aid. They offer a new vision of humanity, one of maximum evolution, connection and accomplishment. That's all great talk, but naught without direction and detail. You will find it here.

I know that *truth* is the ultimate solution to any problem. If you break down what is really wrong with the way life on planet earth is evolving, you will discover truth, or the lack thereof, to be an underlying culprit. If we nurtured a culture of integrity in all things, humanity's light would shine across the universe. Of course, all of this begins with you. You are the light of this world, and you hold the key to an unfolding destiny that will leave all of us bathing in joy. Again, that's why you should read the book.

This book is not a collection of preachy prose or *coulda, woulda, shoulda*. It is a section of a road map that will resonate with you in ways you might not at first be able to explain.

Contained in these pages, you will find wonderful tales of adventure. You will find amazing stories of culture and otherworldy involvement. You will find strategies for survival and recipes for success.

As a producer, to me it almost sounds like some kind of ad for a TV network's new program lineup. Of course, that can't be right, because resolving humanity's challenges in a space of love and having all people rise to their own power and potential could *never* be wrapped in mainstream, exciting phraseology like that...

Of course it could! That's the point. Evolving and becoming a better species that succeeds in its own mission of achieving potential can be every bit as exciting as watching the Santa Monica Pier slip into the ocean in yet another movie about our demise. Elevation is the most exciting thing we could be doing!

No matter where you are in your journey, no matter what you believe, the energy living in this book will touch you on a deep and special level. Enjoy what is has to offer. Then, take its wisdom and go inside. From there you will change the world.

Ronald James left a career in mainstream television to create original films and programs. He has produced over 100 specialty DVDs covering topics such as metaphysics, new science and the paranormal. He is also the author of the forthcoming novel *Messiah* (www.readmessiah.com). More about his work can be found at www.sedonamediacompany.com.

AUTHORS' PREFACE

Over the past several years we have personally witnessed the boiling point on our planet recreating triggers of fear, hopelessness and drama. Through the thousands of listeners and callers to our radio show, *Higher Love*, and during our worldwide personal appearances and journeys, it is evident that the message of empowered free choice is still lacking on a global basis. Despite the true rise in those who seek to anchor a new consciousness that shifts from this energy, the fact remains that the energy of "doom and gloom" is largely considered viable and profitable.

Now is the moment to shift that model...we are at
the sunrise of humanity, the natural evolution from
the experience of a dark night.

We have traveled extensively into the remote highlands of Guatemala and become trusted "insiders" with the highland Maya. We have discovered that *everything* that is unfolding on our planet now is ready to bring forward this new sunrise of humanity, the dawning of our next age, *if* we collectively allow this energy to come forward. We refer to this energy as Passionate Action.

There are clearly two paths ahead of us, and both are challenging. More and more people are beginning to become concerned about 2012 as the boiling point. Recently, we met with a woman for the first time, and she shared that her 17-year-old son had dropped out of high school and was battling with gripping depression. We asked her why, and her answer confirmed the energies we were witnessing and it was not the first time we had heard story like this:

"He figures that his life will end in 2012. He surfs the Net, and all he finds is information telling him that everything will end and that our world will end. His life no longer matters to him, and I don't know what to tell him. He is completely fascinated with the movie *2012* and believes we are destined to die. What should I do?"

What should she do indeed!

This was not our first encounter with high school–age students struggling with the energies that are emerging on our planet now, but it was the first time we encountered this question with the full knowledge of the synergies of both the Ancient Maya and the archangelic realm as a basis to assist with a response.

When one is close with the Maya without trying to exploit them, a cosmology is revealed. When one is able to recognize the cosmic wisdom shared in conjunction with the synergies with the archangelic realm, along with the ancient writings, what comes forward are perennial truths and important revelations for this specific moment in history.

OUR PAST HAS FORECAST OUR NOW

All is not lost. We are ready to move forward.

There will be a new dawn in 2013 if we can heed the messages before us while respecting that each being has the right, through their own filter of loving recognition and presence, to respond as they are called.

Will the rise in polarity and the duplicity in government, along with corporate greed, result in global war and worldwide economic collapse, or will the rising tensions spawn a greater recognition of our interdependence and spiritual commonality and thus minimize the violence? Significant earth changes are coming that will challenge people worldwide.

We also have personally witnessed working prototypes of free-energy machines and solutions to pollution that are feared by the powers that be, for they put public resources back into the hands of the public. Integrity must emerge in the form of new and bold leadership—the victim consciousness that believes a new president within an existing structure will save them is not the solution for the U.S. or the world.

There will be pain on many levels regardless, for birthing a new reality is a cleansing. However, the intensity of that pain and the duration of the discomfort humanity will endure is based upon our collective response over the next seven years. Humanity can follow the path already in place, which will lead to the escalation of war and fear. Or, humanity can cleanse the unproductive structures and stop into a birthing process that will usher in a new era.

2013: Mayan Sunrise makes the case for both outcomes and shares visions that represent both. Bringing this story to print has been a journey of many years and a multitude of experiences. As you journey through this book, you will find yourself experiencing the gift of true adventure, archangelic revelation, scientific invention and thought provoking self-inquiry. This story is the book for this moment.

Everything you are about to read is 100 percent true. We live a simple, clean lifestyle, and the messages and visions we share have not been induced through drugs, herbs or any other outside stimulus. We know that the path of the mystic includes a surrender of waking consciousness into a greater paradigm often misunderstood by the mass consciousness.

The events, people and interactions you are about to experience have not been altered in any way; rather, they have been presented with complete honesty to offer you the richness of the experiences. We have, out of respect for privacy, changed all names of those who are included. It is our sincere intention to honor their many gifts, and their free sharing, while avoiding interference with their personal lives.

While others are still pontificating about the 2012 scenario and its potential, let us move forward and offer the clues for sustaining our world, breaking free of old patterns and benefiting from the wisdom of the indigenous elders in synergy with the archangelic realm and the universal unfoldment before us all at this momentous time.

After all, it is why you chose this planet, at this moment, right now.

As we usher in an extraordinary New Year with a celebratory blue moon, we offer this gift of love and service to you from TOSA Ranch, New Mexico, and TOSA La Laguna Self-Ascension Center, Lake Atitlán, Guatemala.

Sri Ram Kaa & Kira Raa

January 1, 2010

A MESSAGE FROM THE ESSENE BRETHREN

Throughout 2009 we were blessed with the resurrection of the energies of the Essene Brethren and the delivery of the *Lost Books of The Essene*.[1] When this energy first came forward, we were unaware that the Essene were more than the traditionally acknowledged group of beings that are often credited with being the early teachers of Jesus, the Christ.

The Essene brethren offered to us all, through their series of wisdom revelations, a greater context for their presence at this moment on our planet. Here are their exact words:

"This is a powerful moment in your world's
transitionary history.
Transitionary history, is history that is shape-shifted by the
inhabitants of an experience,
who together, co-create that, which will bring forth the
manifest destiny of a great, glorious and luminescent conjunction
of all Divine experience."[2]

We include this message here, at the beginning of the journey of this book, as a gentle and loving reminder to us all. The simple, yet profound message that *we* are the shape-shifters, *we* are the co-creators, and that together we will bring forward our future.

This moment is our divine experience, and the choices before us are within our co-creative dream to manifest. May we all-ways be in harmony with that recognition of our true nature.

Chapter One

WiLL THERE REALLY
BE A 2013?

"YOU ARE AT A MOMENT OF FREEDOM, AND IN THE
MOMENT OF FREEDOM, ALL ENERGY CONVERGES,
ALL MANIFESTATION COMES FORWARD, AND
ALL UNIVERSAL EXPERiENCE CONJOINS."[3]

"My husband sat down with the family last night and told us we needed to be prepared because the world was ending soon," our young Vietnamese waitress said as she stood by our table seeking our response. Her eyes were clearly afraid of what we might say.

What would we say? We were just off the plane, back in Albuquerque from a profound Guatemalan journey, and had arrived at the restaurant seeking a moment of rest and recuperation before making the drive to our ranch.

Kira looked up at her concerned face and asked, "Why does he feel that way?"

"Because he believes what he is seeing and reading on the Internet. He sits there hour after hour finding out everything he can about 2012 and the prophecies and predictions that are posted about that year. He also keeps telling me that the Mayan calendar is ending, and he believes our world is ending with it. We have two young children, and he believes there is no need to save money for college or even pay our debts. He really believes we are all going to die!" She nearly wept as she shared her husband's beliefs. Her underlying subtle energy was screaming to us, "Please tell me this isn't true."

We had been eating at this restaurant every week for years. Our lovely young waitress knew our names, knew our favorite dishes, and in all that time had not ever disclosed anything of her personal beliefs or family life. Nor had we.

Yet here she was on this snowy evening, with virtually no customers in the restaurant except us, instinctively sharing this recent family scenario while still going on about how her husband had called the entire family together. Aunts, uncles, brothers, sisters, grandparents and cousins were all congregated so that he could share with them why they needed to prepare for the coming end of the world.

It was obvious we were not going to get the rest and recuperation we sought at tonight's meal. Instead there was a greater call before us: the reminder that the energy of fear on our planet is rampant, powerful and seductive.

Kira continued, "Have you considered that his beliefs are only one choice before us? Maybe his preoccupation with the end of the world can be a wake-up call to your entire family. There are many choices before us all, and the co-creative power of your thoughts will create what you would like to have in your life."

"Well, I really feel that way, only he would not listen to me or anyone else. His convictions are making me doubt my own beliefs, and I really don't know what to do," she replied. Her energy was now calming down as she allowed herself to start relaxing into a rapport with us just enough to be open to our sharing.

"You might want to begin by intentionally researching the alternative energies around this time. It would also be a gift to let your husband expand his Web search to include the positive predictions and the choices of our future, rather than fixate on the negative. We just arrived home from Guatemala, and we can offer to you that the Maya have no fear of the calendar ending. None. Outsiders who have sought to interpret their calendar have brought forth great fear without a basis in the honest facts. Breathe. Do your best to avoid being preoccupied with fear. You do have a choice here, and your husband is looking at only one option. Help him discover that there are others," Kira assured her.

Sri Ram Kaa smiled and offered, "There are many who believe our world is ending, and there are many who also believe we are entering a golden age. The one thing we can all agree upon is that we are at a time of great shift. What do you really want for your children? That is where you may want to begin focusing, and then bring your husband back into that loving space with you. What you will discover, and be happy to know, is that there is much more waiting for you than just the fear and hype of the end of the world. And, you have to want to find it."

"I'm really glad I shared this with you. I'll do that. I really don't believe my children were born only to die so young and so soon. Okay, let me get your soup!" She smiled, let out a sigh of relief and left our table.

Gazing at each other, we smiled knowingly. This was yet another of many recent encounters that all had a similar energy. The energy of a well-intended individual seeking reassurance from an outside source about a topic they were to afraid to investigate fully. We noticed that all these interactions held in common the fact that people do not trust themselves enough to look at their fears head-on.

Without a doubt, it is the overwhelming preoccupation with fear that has brought us all to this very special moment in our collective history—the moment where we must look, we must investigate and, ultimately, we must trust ourselves.

The Maya have no fear of the calendar ending...none.

❄ ❄ ❄

Throughout the ages, human communities have been guided by the wise elders of their time. While these teachings are often distorted by the beliefs of followers who repeat the information of the elders, kernels of truth remain. One gift that the indigenous elders model for us all is their ability to remain detached from the turbulence of the outer world with its fads and fashions. They listen to their inner guidance and trust it implicitly.

Many prophecies have been shared around the 2012 conversation. Offerings from the Maya, the Hopi, the Zulu, the Dogon, the Cherokee, the Hindu and others all point to a common theme: a transition into a new cycle is occurring right now, and another cycle will begin again in 2012.

The culmination of one cycle can stimulate a sense of loss. During the culmination we tend to forget that there is a sense of a void, and that with the beginning of any new cycle comes an expansive, lifting energy. Thus we are called to be mindful of where we place our attention.

The energy of the third, fourth and fifth dimensions is already here, readily available to the consciousness of all who seek its connection. This can stimulate chaos, for as people anchor their energy and orientation at different frequencies, they embrace the world differently. It is important that the opportunity for energetic expansion be made conscious.

We are in a time unlike any other. Like the wise elders, to walk in peace during such transitions we must widen our gateway to inner communion. At the time of culmination of one way of being, the opportunity for renewal awaits as we engage the beginning of a new cycle. We are free to set in motion a new way of being or to simply repeat the old paradigms and set a repetition in motion.

Now more than ever, we are called to trust our divine nature and experience true clarity. The call is before you to be clear about your choices. Be congruent in your actions and stay focused on the divine in everything you behold. These steps will train your consciousness to align with the deepest levels of truth and the greatest opportunities ahead. This is the path of joy, the other path before us all. The path of joy does not lead toward death or destruction.

Clearly, by recognizing these two paths—joy or fear—we find ourselves at a juncture in the way we express ourselves and experience our lives on this wondrous planet. Are you ready to remember who you are, who you really are? At the foundation of all the fear and hype around 2012, the reality is that you are being called to a new sense of responsibility. It is time to ascend to your authentic self.

The consistent messages from the archangelic realms, as well as Maya mystics, tell us that now is the time for sacred reunification on every level of our being. Between north and south, eagle and condor, man and woman, ego and spirit. This very moment is the time of great opportunity in which everyone is offered a chance to transcend the limited egoic mind and reunite with the soul at the heart of creation.

Our own sacred reunion occurred seven years ago. While on a hike in the Sedona desert just days after meeting Sri in person for the first time, Kira dropped to the ground. Suddenly, Sri found himself dialoging with a being—an archangel[4]—through Kira's body. *"Congratulations, you have found each other again,"* the angel said. It proceeded to detail our mission together should we choose to move forward with it: to deliver nine books to humanity, sharing the path of Self-Ascension at a time when many who had forgotten who they were will be ready to reawaken.

Sri was in shock. He looked deeply into Kira's eyes, radiating brilliant light, and felt his heart melt. He began to cry as this angelic energy spoke through her body. When the angel left, Kira looked at Sri, saw his tears, and said, "What happened? I feel so filled with love and beauty!" From that moment on we have been charged with the gift of assisting humanity—helping all to remember who *you* are. And as the years have been moving rapidly toward the next cycle of the ages, the number of awakened beings on the planet is escalating…rapidly.

NOW IS THE MOMENT FOR YOUR OWN SACRED REUNION WITH THE SELF

For eons, humanity has been depending upon the intellect to meet our challenges. We analyze, scrutinize, mechanize. We do our best to complicate just about everything. We depend upon technology for a sense of power and peace. But you simply will not be able to think your way through the coming years and especially the energy of 2012 and beyond.

You are being called to a new life. It is a life that is far beyond any form of being "mentalized," yet that paradigm is doing its best to assure you of that exact scenario.

You can seek out many writings on 2012. Suddenly, it is popular to write something, anything about this topic and enter the stream of mentalization around its energy. Traditional types of writings provide you with proposed solutions, answers, pictures, predictions; yet it is vital to recognize that such approaches, seeking someone else's ideas from the outer world, will not carry you to your highest potential.

Perhaps your purpose is to walk within a place of trust on the earth—to claim yourself and your inner wisdom—rather than give up your power to someone who has perceived authority or credentials. We only need credentials for constructing machines within the mandates of our societal structures. Your highest degree, your best credential, is *your life*. You are a living, active and precious part of the amazing organism that is humanity.

The blessing of the speeding up of time, the way we are navigating the planet, the way we co-create is that *everything* is designed to assist you to remember the truth of who you are while you still have a body. This is the essence of Self-Ascension, and the coming years will open for you a powerful momentum to fully empower this gift.

This is the powerful moment; the rare and glorious opportunity for extraordinary spiritual expansion.

Many still feel that the change in the air and the future of our world is out of their hands. The truth is, we are *all* still writing the ultimate book on 2012—and beyond—together. Every one of us is a co-author of that book, and collectively we will be finishing and editing that manuscript right up until that moment of divine convergence.

A high priest and *curandera* perform a ceremony at
TOSA La Laguna Self-Ascension Center, Lake Atitlán, Guatemala.

25

A few short years after we were reunited in the desert, we were guided to Guatemala to forge deep and personal partnerships with the Mayan elders of the highlands.[5] One of the many things we delight in is that when we visit with the indigenous people, their simple wisdom evokes deep spiritual reflection.

We are at the moment in time where each one of us gets to have clear vision again if we choose to do so. When you start fully paying attention to everything that the universe is conspiring to help you with, you stop thinking and you start accepting.

2010 is the year of divine acceptance, the rare opportunity to be at the beginning of the larger release of fear and doubt. This energy is especially powerful, as witnessed by the birthing of 2010 with a rare blue moon, which occurred on January 30, 2009, in conjunction with a partial lunar eclipse. This energy opened a multi-dimensional portal for those who sought to embrace it. This portal offered a great gift of clarity through January 15, 2010, when it was anchored by the new moon's full solar eclipse—powerful energy for all to support the expansion.

It is the beginning of remembering who you are, encircling yourself and others in the presence of the true love that transcends all emotions and belief systems. It is the natural return to right action through living right action.

Before you now are the very real, focused energies of fear, ancient prophecies of doom, financial uncertainty and global destabilization. Indeed, there is a darker vision, a cloud that seeks to claim your clarity if you choose to embrace it. This cloud has great strength and momentum on its side. After all, it has been well-fed through the media, mass consciousness, belief systems and, of course, our own fear.

When you are able to go beyond preoccupation, it can be as simple as sincerely declaring, "Enough." Thus you bring forward the greater gift that is yours to unveil—the gift of your authentic clarity. At this moment of overstimulation on all levels of our existence, it is clarity that will gift you with the freedom to clearly see the choices and the energies around you.

Clarity emerges when we relax into our authentic beings and stop showing ourselves distorted points of view. Imagine your life in this moment, right now, with full clarity around the big questions:

- Why am I here?
- What is my purpose?
- What is my highest expression in the world?

And any other question you may wish to bring forward.

It all unfolds when you claim your clarity, which in essence is the empowerment of self-trust, the simple yet profound understanding that the foundation of clarity is trust. Let's look at the word, *clarity*, and expand it so that we can fully embrace this energy of trust. Perhaps you can relax into feeling the mere word *clarity* as a mantra. Just allow yourself to experience the energies that it offers through the greater expansion.

The Clarity Mantra
*I claim love and light in all-ways as I recognize
the infinite and trust myself.*

Let's take a moment and discover this greater energy through the gift of clarity.

C—to Claim   The essence of true clarity is the firm foundation established as you claim the gift of yourself and experience it through the simple, yet sometimes difficult, recognition that you are enough. Recognize lovingly that this world experience is a gift for you to unwrap regardless of the outside issues that may confront you on a day-to-day basis. You woke up today! So it is a good day. Can you begin by claiming that as true for you? This is the essence of claiming, which many refer to as *I AM*. Claim yourself.

L—Love / Light   Our world experience is often filled with emotionality and societal expectations around the energy of love. Yet deep within all beings is an eternal essence of love also known as light. From the scientific perspective, we know that light expands. Then, as love/light, we can know that we are expanding. As part of

this expansion, we seek out new expressions and a multitude of life experiences. These are not meant to affect our love but to enhance it. If you were to bring yourself to 10,000 feet above your life and gaze at all your experiences, you would find your "self," your essence, the love/light that is expressing itself through your life.

A—All-ways   As you claim your foundation as I AM, the love that you are becomes recognized in ways that transcend the mind. This transcendent quality awakens to the joy-filled recognition that everything your life, *everything,* is the expression of your being in form, it is the *all-ways*. Here, on this planet, right now, everyone is expressing everything. Allness is an integral piece of the experience of love/light, and through this recognition we can allow a greater sense of understanding to relax the mind and open the heart. Allow yourself the moment of recognition that you are, in all-ways, expanding love and light.

R—Recognize   The shift away from an external validation system relaxes dependency upon the ego, cultivating an internal trust. This is a lofty goal for many, yet a simple one to attain when we set aside the mind. When we blame, shame, guilt or doubt ourselves or others, we are in a state of denial that refuses to recognize the "we are" (or I AM). This limited state of expression will stop our clarity if we fail to recognize that at the heart of all experience is the Self. Allow yourself to simply recognize *you*, to remember *you*, to acknowledge *you* and to affirm that *you are*. Through this gift of self-recognition, you will rediscover the gift in all experience and smile at the extraordinary clarity that is ready to reveal itself through you.

I—Infinity   Through her two near-death experiences, Kira Raa was gifted with the absolute undeniable knowing that we are infinite beings that do not ever die. While we pray that you do not ever need to die to know this truth, recognizing your immortality is a vital piece of removing all doubt of your life experience. You are a limitless being, so it is only natural you will have limitless experiences[6] in harmony with your creative ability to manifest them while here on this planet. So how do limitless beings lose their clarity? Through the limiting belief systems perpetuated in a world that seeks to keep you unclear. To accept your limitless nature will open the doorway beyond your

limiting beliefs. You are free to have an amazing life the moment you reclaim your limitless nature.

T—Trust   Lets face it, we live in a world that teaches us not to trust or to qualify our trust. This element ties in directly to the limiting beliefs that also hold back our infinite nature. There is a great value in learning discernment and a greater sense of freedom when we recognize that discernment is the filter to navigate this world while trust is the foundation of our being. Trust is our divine nature. When we allow trust back into our lives, we find a greater sense of harmony, joy and enthusiasm for life. We call to ourselves others who are free from the limiting beliefs of distrust and discover that our discernment is trustworthy. This is a monumental moment of clarity and pivotal for humanity as we call forth our discernment and trust to pave the way.

Y—Yourself!   When was the last time you gazed into a mirror and honestly enjoyed the *you* that was greeting your gaze? To fully claim your clarity and allow the gift of true vision of the world experience around you to unfold, it must begin right in that mirror, with you gazing at you. Whatever it takes, whatever you need, wherever you must go, commit to doing it as long as the end result is your comfortable, joy-filled, confident gaze returned to you in that mirror. *You* are that important. Your participation in the world is not passive; it is active through your thoughts, your actions and your presence. It *does* all begin with you. It is a journey you started the day you were born and one you live every second you draw breath. Claim yourself through the recognition that everything, every life experience, every moment is simply a reminder that your clarity is waiting patiently. Once you rediscover it, so is your amazing life.

Clarity is the energy of a consciousness freed from fear.

The importance of a worldwide epidemic of clarity cannot be stressed enough. It is a vital component for navigating the times ahead. It is your greatest weapon against a time of misinformation, intentional misdirection and conflicting views and actions.

The bottom line is that there *will* be a 2013. How we all experience that time—and beyond—is the greater experience before us now.

Throughout this book, we offer to you a variety of perspectives, revelations and thought-provoking stimuli to assist your clarity. We introduce you to amazing people we have met along the way and invite you to relax into a paradigm shift that may at times challenge you about your origins, your life and your world experience.

Each of these revelations will enhance your clarity if you allow them to do so. The choice is yours. It has always been yours, and now is your moment.

Will you choose to focus on the darker vision, the cloud?
Or will you help usher in the time of clarity?
Will you choose, now, to remember who you are?

Chapter Two

GUATEMALA: THE FINAL PIECE OF THE PUZZLE

"IT IS YOUR TIME TO REJOICE, CELEBRATE AND REMEMBER!"[7]

After five years of constant travel, nearly a thousand archangelic in-soulments, radio shows and workshops, that very special moment arrived: we were going on vacation! Or so we thought. Once again the gift of the universe, keeping us on a need-to-know basis, came forward with all the power, magic and wisdom that one could ever dream of.

How does one even begin to share the magnitude that comes forward when the universe has called and the answers have revealed themselves? Following the heart path that has led us to Guatemala is a continually unfolding adventure deep within the Land of Eternal Spring[8] that is offering a blessing now for all humanity.

Whenever you are called to visit a sacred site that was a place of importance in past times, a sense of awe and wonder awakens inside you. And when that site is endowed with something even more fundamental, you discover that this essence is calling to your soul, and the effect of being there is even more pronounced.

Central America is the heart of the Americas. Guatemala is centrally located within the heart of Central America. It is literally the heart of the heart. Once you touch its soil, your heart can only do one thing—respond! Through our journeys we have discovered why this little-known, frequently misunderstood country stands pivotal in the forward journey of humanity.

Our many visitations with both the Highland Maya and the archangelic realms have revealed a synergy unfolding before us. Such interactions have stimulated opportunities such as:

- Walking through life-threatening illness / energies;
- In-depth communication with UFOs over Lake Atitlán;
- Clearing an ancient burial site and uncovering ancient "Mayan secrets";
- Meeting with extraordinary beings who are holding extraordinary light energy;
- Holding Mayan grandmothers in our arms while we cried and remembered;
- Entering ancient, secret Mayan altars and receiving direct transmissions from the high priests; and
- Uncovering—or more accurately, rediscovering—the sacred land that has held the heartbeat of 2012 and future of humanity.

As we begin to share this journey with you, please recognize that none of "us" are ever in control. There is a greater order influencing our lives. We thought that we had this journey all planned out. We had carefully attended to every detail, and from the moment we stepped on the first plane in Albuquerque, NM, the universe gently reminded us that "they" had other plans and did everything in their power to continually reinforce this fact.

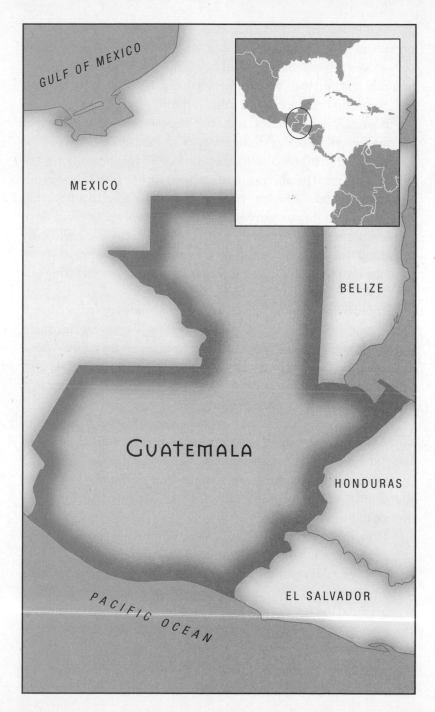

Our initial trip to Ft. Lauderdale, where we would stop for the night, was to be a total of five hours. We planned to enjoy time with our wonderful students as part of our Golden Ray[9] tele-class, have a leisurely rest and then buoyantly arrive in Guatemala City the next day. Sounds relaxed and enjoyable . . . right?

It was 17, yes 17, hours later after stepping onto that plane that we finally arrived at our destination in Ft. Lauderdale. We had no idea at the time that accepting the number 17 was actually part of the unfoldment. The universe had stepped in, our schedule was out the window, and we had no choice but to surrender to a flow that had other plans for our journey. We were suddenly in the middle of a much larger revelation for the future of our planet and could only grab presence and hold on as it was revealing itself before us! We let go of the idea were on a relaxing vacation. We were surrendering our physical, mental and emotional boundaries.

The extreme stress and poor conditions on the plane were enough to push our bodies to the brink of illness. Within hours we were coughing as our lungs congested and we began to lose our vitality. After a brief three hours of rest, we were on the next plane to Guatemala City, where we had about an hour to regain our presence before our first meeting. Our bodies were beginning to really speak to us.

Despite the physical weakness, we were overjoyed to meet with an extraordinary group of light workers who had invited us to join them at a sacred site in Guatemala City. This group was organized by Andre, an amazing man whom we lovingly recognize as a sacred grandfather of light, a pure heart who has dedicated his life to the service of the world.

Honoring us with this time of deep and loving connection, his tiny living room was filled with many from other dimensions, along with a Mayan elder grandmother and her daughter, who had walked a great distance over several days just to come meet with us. There was great loving recognition and a pledge of solidarity to continue the work of Self-Ascension in Guatemala and tears of welcome to this sacred portal.

Our bodies had seemingly gone into stasis during this important first meeting. Within a few short hours we were on our way to Lake

Sri Ram Kaa, Kira Raa and Andre share a moment of love and recognition
with our Mayan grandmother, her daughter and a
Guatemalan supporter of self-ascension.

Atitlán, to be there the next night for the full moon lunar eclipse. The
long yet beautiful drive was not an easy task as we wound our way
through the hairpin turns and dizzying countryside. Yet the energy
of anticipation grew with each turn.

We arrived at Lake Atitlán. Her beauty was in all ways breath-
taking. The majestic volcanoes, the perfectly blues skies and the energy
of water, air, earth and spirit were palpable. The small B&B we had
arranged to stay at for the first night was lovely and private. It unveiled
another piece of the puzzle that was rapidly coming together. We had
been excited to stay here for this night of transition before venturing out
farther around the lake. The proprietor, whose facility only had three
bedrooms, was eager to make us a vegan meal. Since we were occupy-
ing two of the rooms, we found the solitude welcoming and restful.

What the proprietor had neglected to share when we reserved
our rooms was that the third bedroom was occupied by her dying
father, whose deathbed was in full view through the hallway window

A view of two of the volcanoes at Lake Atitlán.

of his room. The energy of death and release was so tangible that Kira fell into bed and began to slip away from the world. What we did not realize in the moment was that she was assisting the man in the next door bedroom to release fear by joining him on his journey of transition. Kira's experience with "the other side" offered a gift of guidance and the release of fear to this man who was confused about making his transition. Simultaneously, she was receiving greater assistance from the realms beyond this world to prepare for what lay ahead in the next 24 hours.

Staring up at the stars that evening from the shores of Lake Atitlán, with the magnificence of the three volcanoes painted against the backdrop of an evening sky, transcends words. The presence of ancient Maya blends into the everyday lives of all those who call the lake home makes for a heady blend of modern and mystical. There is a reason this extraordinary lake has been called the most beautiful in the world by poets, scholars and travelers alike. Yet, it rises above the beauty of nature. It is that rare synergy of Gaia, sun, moon, air and spirit fully empowered and fully present without hesitancy as to her full essence and splendor.

Some of the lake towns are busy with tourists, restaurants, shops and hotels. Shamans-for-hire are easily obtained, and the spirit of the '60s is alive and well. Yet just beyond this façade, around the remote reaches of the lake, one is able to easily discover the "heart" of the authentic Atitlán experience.

Still between two worlds in the morning, it was challenging to get Kira out of bed and functional. We assisted her to board the small village boat we needed to transverse the lake. The cool winds of the open-air boat cooled her high fever and comforted her very weakened physical presence. Arriving at our destination on the other side of the lake opened a portal of powerful Mayan reconnection. It felt as if we were walking between two worlds. We were at times dizzy and distant, yet aware that a preparation of some form was at hand.

The gusty winds and dark clouds were accumulating all through-out the day, foreshadowing the evening ahead. Settling in at the house, we were all taken by the small, obviously starving kitten that was eager to jump into our laps and purr. Yet each time the caretaker came close, she would jump, run and hide. Our hearts realized that along with the imminent lunar eclipse, the kitten was part of the reason we were at this location. Yesterday we had touched the energy of decay and release; today we connected with the hopes of a kitten.

Kira spent the entire afternoon in bed, doing her best to stay connected, and by now Sri Ram Kaa was also feeling the drain of energy that was trying to claim his vitality. Early in the evening it began to rain, and with each passing hour the rain was more powerful until it reached a drenching apex and released a powerful downpour. We began feeding this wonderful little kitten, keeping it safe and dry, knowing that the entire property was being cleansed in all aspects. The physical fatigue, together with the energy upon us, made surrender the only viable choice.

At the time of the lunar eclipse we began a ceremony in the house, as the storm's intensity kept us from going outside. The sky was very dark—not a star, certainly not the moon—yet the energy of the eclipse was tangible and increasing. As three of us sat in a sacred circle, our meditation deepened, our tones aligned and within what felt like an instant, the revelations began pouring forth.

The revelations were beyond any earthbound connection we had known before. Yet before us was what felt like a movie playing, revealing ancient lifetimes we had shared in this environment, familial connections, ancient campfires, swirling smoke, powerful ceremonies, flashes of light, remembrances of commitments and promises made, along with the revelation of a lost city that was hidden beneath the waters of the lake. We each celebrated our experience, and as the evening wore on Kira once again slipped out of this dimension as we just sat, held presence and trusted the process. The ancient ones who spoke through her offered celebration that the fires of community were being ignited again.

We were now beyond the lunar eclipse and our mystical interactions through the stormy night. Our fevers were ever present as our lungs became weaker and weaker. Today we were being called to a property that we learned was for sale on the far corner of the lake… still remote and hidden from most, at the deepest, cleanest area of the water. It was calling us, and we knew to follow the call.

Climbing into our boat and leaving our one-night cosmic experience behind, we felt unusually exhilarated despite our physical condition, and the cool air off the lake was comforting to the high fevers. We felt a "bridge" being created over the lake, as if we were traveling in another dimension, as we passed by all three volcanoes on our way to the other side.

As we approached what would later become TOSA La Laguna Self-Ascension Center, profound visions of the Goddess of the Lake began for Kira. We were all filled with tears and overwhelmed by the energy that was making itself so visible. Perhaps the fevers and the weakened condition of our bodies were to prepare us for this moment, as the ascended guardians were making themselves known.

Landing at the boat dock on the property, we began to climb the lush stone trails carved into the mountainside. We felt drawn to the original Mayan sauna on the property. Similar to a Native American Sweat Lodge, the Mayan sauna is used to induce trance-like states of higher consciousness to connect with divine guidance.

The rock dome appeared before us on the trail as Kira began to swoon and was caught by Sri and our guide. The closer we came to the sauna, the more powerfully we experienced swirling energy. Upon reaching the summit where it was perched, we had to stop, catch our breath and align with the potent energy.

As we opened the door, our hearts were filled with joy. Beautiful symbols were carved into the sides of the sauna. Sri took a moment to photograph the interior through the small doorway and his digital camera took several pictures within a second of time. We were delighted that they actually captured the energy portal we had all been experiencing.

If you gaze at the first picture of the sauna, you can see clearly that the portal is very visible, and just a second later, it shows a clear shot of the inside. This picture also shows that the center is completely clear once you are inside the sauna, yet the energy being held in this area was present for us to experience.

Later that day, we said goodbye to our beloved friend and checked into a hotel to collapse into bed. For four days we were in that room, not sure when our energy would stabilize enough to leave it. Each day and night we were filled with powerful visions and experiences that are still too challenging to put into words. During this time we stepped into other worlds and received great gifts of energy, knowing it would be shared later.

With only two days left before we were scheduled to return to the United States, we began to feel our physical energy returning to us. That evening we received a fateful call from a friend:

"You must come with me very early tomorrow morning to meet with the high priest of the Maya." The request came from another dear friend already living at Lake Atitlán.

"I don't know if Kira can make it," Sri responded, yet we both knew we had to make this divine appointment, so we went ahead and made the arrangements.

Early the next morning we stood on the corner, climbed onto the vegetable truck and headed high into the mountains overlooking the lake. We off-loaded ourselves outside a small alley lined with old adobe walls and walked into another world—truly another dimension from which we would never be the same.

Above: A tangible portal of dimensional energy caught on film at the ancient Mayan Sauna at TOSA La Laguna. Right: This photo, taken just a second later, shows a calm interior to experience the portal of connection.

Standing by a large, very old metal door were two elders from the Mayan community whose approval to enter was mandatory. Since we do not speak Cakchiquel[7], it was the tip of an old straw hat, large toothless smiles, and flowing waving hands that motioned us to go in.

Walking through the door, we entered a dark, small room lined with two long benches along each wall and an eclectic altar at the front. The room was filled with the smell of copal, and smoke hung in the air from recent offerings. The energy was at one moment extraordinary and the next overwhelming.

Out of the darkness from the back of the room, the high priest emerged through a small door we had not even noticed. He motioned for our friend to come join him at his small desk in the back. We sat tenuously on the very small benches made for Mayas, not tall Americans.

We watched with fascination as he would gaze up at us, then arranged beans on his small desk and scattered crystals with them. Keeping his gaze fixed, he would nod his head, speak in his native language, and then continue his divination without looking up. Our friend only spoke Spanish, so until he was ready to share, we all simply sat, watched and felt the energy of this process.

About five minutes later he said something in Spanish to our friend, who turned around and asked us to come join them at the small desk. We were greeted with love and joy. As a celebration of our connection and our time together, we gifted the high priest with a crystal and corn necklace Kira Raa had made by hand as a gift from the world of the eagle in connection with the cosmic life force. He was delighted to receive this gift and promptly put it on with a broad smile.

Our friend began translating on our behalf. She explained that he had been performing his final "reading" to see if we were the ones he had seen prior to coming and asked if we had any questions. We did not. How could you have a question in the moment of divine connection?

Satisfied with our answer, he said it was important for us to do ceremony together and that the moment had arrived. We had thought his reading was the ceremony. He stood and motioned for us to walk through the small metal door he had entered through. As tall Americans, we stooped low to enter through this ancient metal door. At that moment we felt like Dorothy[11] stepping into the world of color for the first time. Everything began to shift forever.

We knew we had been called to Guatemala for many reasons. We were fairly certain we had found TOSA La Laguna and confirmed many of our own visions. Yet, what was waiting behind the door was beyond anything our minds could have ever created.

As we adjusted fully to the light in the large room, we were acutely aware of the energy of floating.[12] We were standing in what must have been one of the last preserved, original Mayan altars that has been standing before the invasion of the conquistadors in the 1500s. To our left were stone and jade carved relics—many dozens of jaguars, birds, gods, serpents and more, each carving so clearly ancient and so alive with energy that it was if they were speaking to us.

Sri Ram Kaa jumped at the feeling that one of the jaguars was walking around him. We were still adjusting to our environment and had not even noticed that our beloved high priest was already busily preparing the ceremony. With his large machete, he was opening long bundles of handmade copal briquettes, each wrapped in dried corn husks. There were supplies of candles, flowers, chocolates, small pieces of pine wood, copal and other items that we could not identify.

The altar was unlike anything we had ever seen before. It was clear that very few outside of the Mayan community had witnessed this extraordinary architecture, since it has never really been described. The humble energy that poured through us was tangible. Of course, photography was out of the question. Part of the reason we were taken into the confidence of the elders was our sincere commitment to share their story and honor their traditions.

The altar was approximately 18 feet around at its bottom layer. The circles of carved stone sat upon one another like a three tier wedding cake. At each of the four directions, as in the Mayan cross, an entrance cut into the stone led underneath the altar. Our priest quickly and effortlessly brought his supplies to the topmost level to build the ceremonial fire that would confirm all of inner visions.

At the sides of the altar stood two tall stone pillars, each towering about 15 feet high and carved with the symbols of the Mayan calendar.

The energy was overwhelming, and simply standing was becoming a challenge. At that moment he motioned that we were ready to begin by shoving candles into our hands, giving us a small handmade corn mat to kneel on and starting an ancient Mayan chant.

Within moments the entire chamber was filled with wafting copal and thick smoke as the fire grew to extraordinary heights. Prayers and offerings were uttered by the priest, and the fire danced atop the altar. Chanting and adding ceremonial offerings one at a time, he was obviously reading the fire in the same way one would carefully inspect a sacred object to ascertain its gifts. Our vibrational fields were heightened, and we had totally lost all sense of time and space, when suddenly a hand was on Kira's back.

So entranced by the energy of the fire and the power of the ceremony, Kira had somehow managed to begin to walk into the flames. It was as if an outside energy had called her to physically enter to fire, to become one with it, and she was completely unaware that she was standing in the flames until Sri Ram Kaa pulled her out.

Dazed, yet not fully in the world of density, Kira turned to the high priest, who greeted her with a buoyant smile and they began to communicate in a language that neither Sri Ram Kaa nor our beloved friend understood, yet the messages pouring forth were clear to all of us. They were far beyond the mind's paradigms, yet understanding prevailed.

Then the high priest's eyes turned to pure, crystalline, liquid light. Kira Raa locked into his gaze, and it was as if the two of them traveled light years beyond this world and back again within an instant, eternity revealed and revelations understood.

As the fire began to diminish and the smoke started clearing, we all simply gazed at one another with reverence, love and the tears of joy that come from deep within the soul. Simply connecting with the smoldering embers, the high priest gazed at Sri and Kira and said, "You are here to connect the rainbow bridge. The land you seek to reclaim is a destiny fulfilled. For many years there have been wanderers who have not understood what it was they sought. This new portal of energy that will be found at your end of the bridge will reveal once again that which has been lost, and is now reawakening."

"Will you help us? Will you come to the land and assist with the reawakening?" whispered Kira, barely able to speak at all.

"Yes, I will. I have been waiting for this moment, and it is a happy day when a vision is fulfilled," the high priest responded as he held out his arms and embraced Kira Raa.

He then turned and embraced Sri Ram Kaa and our dear friend. As we left, he was already cleaning the altar in preparation for his next ceremony. In the small room where we had sat earlier, villagers eagerly waited to be with him. They showed up without appointments, walking in with their offerings for the high priest—corn, tortillas, live chickens or whatever they felt was appropriate for the requests they were making.

Practicing high priests are healers and mentors. They are the ones who train shamans. Honored and respected, they often come from a long lineage of Mayan priests who were fortunate enough not to be annihilated during the ethnic cleansing of the civil war.

They do not seek fame. They choose not to learn English. Many of them do not even speak Spanish. They have no desire to be sought after by those who are merely fascinated with who they are. They have no desire to mix with those who are not Maya. They are not for hire like the many self-styled priests and shamans who are easily found on the Internet. They live simply and stay connected to the balance of all life. They work 18 hours a day, every day, and smile through it all.

Living their lineage authentically, they wake up very early every morning in complete and humble service to their communities. Those who seek them out come for every reason imaginable—healing of illnesses, fertility, spiritual connection, ceremonies to consecrate stages of life, help with common issues and many more.

We have come to know high priests on a personal basis now. They have allowed us unprecedented access to their lives, their remote villages and their most private ceremonies.

When we ask them about their calendar, the traditional Mayan calendar, they always smile. Often their response to a "2012" question is as simple as "It is the return of more light. There will be no need for time the way we have known, so why hold on to that which no longer serves?"

On this very special day when we first shared at the sacred, secret altar, we were in our own altered state as we emerged from the small, hidden alleyway and found our way back into the brilliant sun. Once again hopping into the back of a vegetable truck and feeling very tall, it was as if a positive gateway had reignited. We recognized that yet another portal of positive connection to the universal flow was ready to anchor on our planet and that the revelations of this gift had just begun.

This was just the beginning of our discovery of the heart of Guatemala and the heart of humanity. Had anyone told us that these energies awaited in Guatemala, we would have quickly said, "Guate— who?" Yet, from the eyes of the awakened, one clearly starts to make the connections that go back millennia and helped keep the energy of the universal heart safe so that it could come forward with brilliant resurrection at this moment in history.

※ ※ ※

CO-CREATING MIRACLES AT THE TIME OF RESURRECTION

"You are all family. You are all of oneness. It is when you join together in this conscious knowing as a family of action, that the miracles you seek abundantly appear."

—ARCHANGEL ZADKIEL

The work of the archangelic realm is one of everyday miracles, which come in many forms and offer each being the incredible gift of knowing without doubt why they are on the planet and how to express this profound energy without any imposed limits.

When your love, energy and support become focused, clear and harmonized—your divine purpose for being—you enter into the true nature of the universe, joy-filled expansion. As we gaze at the times ahead, it is important to call forth the gift of our miracle nature. It is within you to create miracles in your life, yet most people's world experience has done its best to convince us that this is simply not possible.

We have witnessed such miracles firsthand. We have been blessed to received e-mails and letters and calls from hundreds of others who have created miracles too. As part of your journey through this book, we would like to invite you to be part of a Miracle Team.[13]

Each week, we lead a world-clearing ceremony on Sunday afternoon. This includes clearing scattered energies from throughout the world through a process gifted to us directly from the archangelic realm. During this powerful, sacred ceremony, messages for the Miracle Team are received and then distributed to team members for weekly action and manifestation as they see fit.

As more and more of the Miracle Team reunite in love and service, we are all able to contribute in a much more expansive role in the great awakening. The Miracle Team is a vital and positive energetic gift to this planet, assisting many through the global shifts upon us at this time in history.

So, as our gift to you, at the end of each chapter you will find a symbol with the text, "Your Miracle Moment." These very special messages were brought forth for the Miracle Team and can empower your miracle energy if you call them in. Allow yourself to read the message, put your book down, take in a deep breath and receive. You may want to read the message more than once. You may find a particular message especially captivating, then earmark it, highlight it, return to it often.

You are already participating in creating the greatest miracle of all: the return to our harmony as inhabitants of this beautiful world. Now it is your moment to claim your miracle presence and allow it to unfold in your life at any moment you choose.

Your Miracle Moment

This Miracle Message is from the Benevolent Ones:[14]

Beloved custodians of the crystalline light in form, we celebrate thee with joy and recognition of the eternal presence you illuminate so well! Today, as with each day, is the moment of Divine Memory incarnate. Today, your heart fills with the swell of love that flows like an ocean coming home to shore. With each homecoming there is a reunion of love and light that dances with the stars and understands eternity.

May today be your homecoming as you gaze at the sun, dazzle with the light and simply remember you are eternity…and you are the moment. To practice this gift often ignites the energy of eternal light and homecoming for your world and for those who are connected to your world.

This energy transcends all words and calls forth your Divine empowerment through ever greater alignment with your Divine Memory. A breath is a powerful moment, and eternity is contained within each one. Let your breath be full, let it be allowing, and may you In-joy the In-lightenment of each miracle that is manifest for you…now.

Chapter Three

THE WISDOM
PROPHECY
CONVERGENCE

"THERE IS SIMPLY THE DIVINE EXPERIENCE
PLAYING ON A FIELD OF LOVE."[15]

The rainy season in Guatemala is particularly mystical. Each morning the sun rises and fills the sky with light, renewal and hope. Everyone busily takes advantage of this gift, knowing that by the afternoon a dependable downpour will engulf everything and virtually all activity will cease for hours. Many roads instantly become impassable, the sky is dark and lofty, and the rain is extraordinary. From this daily experience of brilliant sun and intense rain rises the fog.

Beauty created through rain and fog at TOSA La Laguna.

The word *fog* does not accurately or fully describe the mystical energy that consumes the Guatemalans during this season, it simply *is*. You experience the fog and the many gifts of the rain in innumerable ways—fertile earth, bountiful plants, pristine forests and a rich heritage of people who have become one with the sun, one with the rain and one with the mystical energies of the fog.

To fully appreciate the ancient mystical energy in Guatemala, you must either give way to the rain and the fog or be consumed by it. Either experience is available, and sometimes you are engulfed while you are flowing, while at the same time you recognize that there is only one experience occurring, and everything you may perceive is consumed by it.

This energy had called us to Guatemala quite suddenly. Little did we know that yet another profound and important revelation for the continuation of humanity would reveal itself during our days there.

We arrived in Guatemala City one morning when the sky was unusually brilliant. Everyone was commenting on the sudden break from the rains and the unusual amount of sunshine. We made our way deep into the city to meet with those who were paving the way for our return to the highlands and the ancient Maya.

Guatemala City is a city of contrasts. Thriving metropolitan sky-scrapers, hotels, banks and businesses set against powerful volcanoes and stunning landscapes. Both businessmen in suits and Maya in native dress mingle on the sidewalks. In a country with only one major city, everything exists here. Simply navigating the streets in a car is a history lesson that can take your breath away and an introduction to the vast energies that thrive in this Land of Eternal Spring.

On our second day in the city, feeling drawn to revisit the extraordinary archeological site Kaminal Juyu, yet lacking time to do so, we decided to journey to Antigua. Once the capital of all Central America, today it stands as a bridge between the city and the countryside. Reminders of colonial Central America (many of which were toppled by powerful earthquakes) stand everywhere in Antigua, and the central square teems with music, people, ceremony and magic.

We lovingly call this town "the city behind walls" because each street is long, narrow, cobblestoned and lined with tall, often colorful walls. Not much to see if you choose not to venture beyond them! This is part of the reason the main square is now largely populated by

Early morning mountain fog in the mystical Mayan highlands.

tourists. It is the one spot in town where entrances are open and commerce is king. Yet, the experience of the central square is upstaged by the hidden treasures behind the walls. The energy of colonial Central America is rich, and the blend of Mayan and Christian mysticism is everywhere.

The rains begin, and everyone is once again behind the walls as a quietude comes forth that beckons greater connection. In this moment a hammock seems perfect, and the extraordinary variety of flowers, plants and trees smile in the afternoon shower. The smell of green is everywhere, along with the smoke from many cooking fires being lit around the town. It is not difficult to find the mysticism here. One only need be available for it.

The ancient Maya revered jade and used it ceremonially in many extraordinary ways. Guatemalan jade is found in approximately 25 different shades, each radiating a unique energy. Antigua is the pinnacle of experience of Guatemalan jade, and galleries are everywhere, exhibiting modern jewelry designs and reproductions of ancient pieces, and stories of ancient Maya go with them.

Sri and Kira experiencing love and peace at an ancient site at Antigua.

At the end of a long corridor, behind the wall, the garden appears.

As we were drawn into a small gallery on a side street, we found ourselves swirling with immense crown energy while communing with several of the jade masks in their sealed glass cases. The exact replication of these masks from the Mayan originals in conjunction with the energy of the jade led us to the next stop on our journey.

Another dear friend, a native Guatemalan, told us of a local "Indiana Jones" who lived in Antigua and made his living in Mayan artifacts. Seeing our immediate connection and response to the masks, she asked if we would like to visit her friend. "Of course," we responded, and she was on the phone in moments. "Indiana" (his real name is withheld due to the nature of his antiquity dealings), was home and could see us at 4 p.m. We were delighted at the synchronicity of it. The rest of the day seemed to crawl toward our meeting.

When we arrived at Indiana's home, the rain had just started coming down heavily. Doing our best to stay dry under a small umbrella, we were greeted at the street by an armed guard in a small room with bars across the windows. After a brief conversation, the large gates swung open and, as is typical in Antigua, behind the high walls was a stunning courtyard with doors to several beautiful apartments. A warm, lovely young woman waved to us with a smile as we entered Indiana's apartment and began to walk up the stairs. The ancient energy was tangible and immediate.

Each step was a history book of ancient Mayan culture. Walking up the steps, it was necessary to avoid the stunning artifacts resting on each one. Rich, lavish oil paintings from colonial churches hung on the walls. Each artifact radiated its story. We could feel our hearts beat as our breath became shallow and our crown chakras began to swirl.

Arriving at the top of the steps, we entered into Indiana's main living room and were greeted by a pair of picture-perfect carved stone Mayan guardians estimated to be from 2500 BC. They literally overpowered our ability to speak as we were handed fresh squeezed pineapple juice. As we acclimated to the experience of this "museum," Indiana himself joined us. He was tall, thin and American in appearance, yet surprisingly Guatemalan in his demeanor. Warm and welcoming, he was outspoken, yet reserved. We enjoyed our juice as he shared his stories of 14 years in Guatemala and how he had come to be an antiquities dealer. The charming elegance in his sharing, combined with his extraordinary knowledge of the ancient Mayan culture, was a treat to experience.

As we toured each room of his apartment, the energies kept building. His wealth of knowledge seemed limitless. We held ancient pottery in perfect condition, discovered the many different ways that fakes are produced and distributed and went through thousands of years of Mayan culture in three rooms and three hours. Even as we share this with you, the words are not adequate to fully describe the depth of this experience. From the energetics of ancient times to a university education in archaeology, information was flooding into us.

It was in the last room that the energy of the ancient artifacts found an overwhelming voice. We heard chanting, sound and harmony and smelled fire as we did our best not to fall over from the extraordinary spinning energies that surrounded us. Indiana indicated that this room had the oldest artifacts. As he was casually sharing with us, he threw open the doors of a large antique armoire with literally hundreds of stone artifacts inside. He started pulling them out one by one, and as he did, a particular artifact called to us from the sideboard.

"He" was a simple, pre-classic figure lovingly sitting there on his altar with his hands across his heart and his legs in mediation posture. His energy was strong and present, and once we each touched him, putting him down became impossible. It was as if he had been waiting for this moment to reveal the mystical revelations he had witnessed and held guarded for so long. The doors had opened for his revelations.

As our dear friend held this "babe" in her arms, Indiana placed a small, similar-looking artifact into Kira Raa's hands. "His" face was cosmic, and his arms were also across his heart. Once in Kira's hands, the stone started heating up intensely and came alive as the color of the stone literally flushed back illuminating the facial features ever more. Tears were in Kira's eyes, and she was unable to do anything but be present with the consciousness that was seeking to be heard and remembered.

Indiana told us that both of these special artifacts were pre-classic, from approximately 300 BC, and that both came from Kaminal Juyu.[16]

The revelation confirmed that this had been a divine appointment. Only 48 hours from the solstice, we would be leaving shortly for Lake Atitlán to rejoin with our Mayan connections. To bring these important energy holders with us felt preordained.

Hesitant to ask, since most of the artifacts in Indiana's apartment were worth many thousands of dollars, Kira Raa wondered aloud what Indiana would want for the stone carving she was holding. He gazed thoughtfully at Kira, fascinated with her way of interacting with

The two special artifacts sharing sacred time together.

the artifact. He brought his hand to his chin, took a deep breath and, with a wave of the same hand, said, "I cannot charge you, it is obvious you are to have it. Please unlock its wisdom and accept it as my gift."

Kira Raa could not hold back the tears as she offered Indiana a hug of appreciation and gratitude.

Our Guatemalan companion also knew that the stone babe she had been cradling in her arms was another part of the experience before us at the lake. When she asked Indiana what it cost, he made it available at a price so low that this too became part of the next stage of our journey.

It was late in the day when we said farewell to Indiana, and we had an early morning ahead of us, traveling to the lake in time for the solstice. Yes, there was a role that these artifacts had been asked to fill, for it was during that first ceremony at the lake that the profound revelations of the ascended masters at Lake Atitlán first came forward and the abode that had been hidden for eons was opened.

☀ ☀ ☀

We are at the time of the great convergence. We are offered a plethora of traditions that seek a common ground together: the Mayan calendar, the predictions of Nostradamus, the Bible's Book of Revelations, the Kali Yuga and Hindu prophecy, the Hopi prophecies, the Dogon and many more. Each foretells a great transition. Some predict strife, and others great abundance and peace. Our journeys to Guatemala gave us the opportunity to live a revelation, to be in the energy of an alignment that is coming to the forefront.

What we have discovered is that when you overlay the profound information that has been revealed to us through the archangelic realm along with the present-day revelations from the Maya, you discover the answer to the question, What does it all mean?

There is one common denominator in all of these prophecies. Our collective consciousness is being prepared to accept, and be receptive to, a significant paradigm shift.

As you read the declaration above, allow yourself to simply take in a deep breath and ponder the following questions:

- What if the context of our earthly experience is being folded into a greater context?
- What if our consensus reality is experiencing new frequencies that will alter our paradigms forever?
- Is humanity prepared to fully move forward with all that is converging around us?

Often a moment of great opportunity stimulates fear, and people step away. Others step through the void and embrace the new.

Density consciousness, the first layer in the Pyramid of Spiritual Awakening below, is the vibrational stratum of mass consciousness, characterized by fear and self-preoccupation. The ego arises to deal with fear and is strengthened by these separation energies. The ego is a product of separation, a refraction of you.

When we open up to the recognition that a greater or galactic energy is penetrating our psyche, our holographic reality, this energy is of a higher frequency than density. The cosmic stream of energy, unrefracted by the egoic preoccupations of Density Consciousness, offers an opportunity to remember unity. Unity and love offer a resolution to the fear underlying Density Consciousness, however, higher vibrational streams of energy are often feared. Unity and oneness are initially felt as a death of the ego.

- What if we are loved beyond our own comprehension of love?
- What if we are being awakened gently through undeniable inter-dimensional experiences?
- Are we listening?
- Are we ready?

Perhaps the purpose of all prophecy and spiritual phenomenon is to place a seed into our consciousness, a gift of love that awakens our profound co-creative power at this moment of transformational choice. We are being awakened from density consciousness. The transition from density consciousness to ascension awareness (the third tier in the Pyramid of Spiritual Awakening) means we must navigate our spiritual activism which brings forth some challenges along the way. We call this stratum ascension awareness, an ascended perspective grounded in love. In ascension awareness our alignment is with our soul, not our personality.

How do we release the grip of density consciousness respectfully while also honoring the truth of our core energy? When we sincerely embrace our divine presence and recognize that we are the ones creating our experience, frustration ceases.

Most people fear an uncertain future. That is, uncertainty creates anxiety. For the density ego, that uncertainty is to be avoided. The divine self is anchored in the peace of its beingness and thus the flux and flow of the outer world provide experiences and opportunities to serve and witness. There is no inherent anxiety—flux and flow are no threat.

Thus, the greater context of prophecy is to prepare consciousness. That can be a kind thing. To have some warning about a potential challenge presents us with the opportunity to more calmly review our resources and options. This increases the odds that we will respond in a better way.

Sometimes a specific prophecy is popularized with a hidden motivation or agenda. Perhaps the purpose of the prediction is to manipulate consciousness toward a desired outcome based upon an external control mechanism. By stimulating fear, a prophecy can become a probability if enough people focus on it.

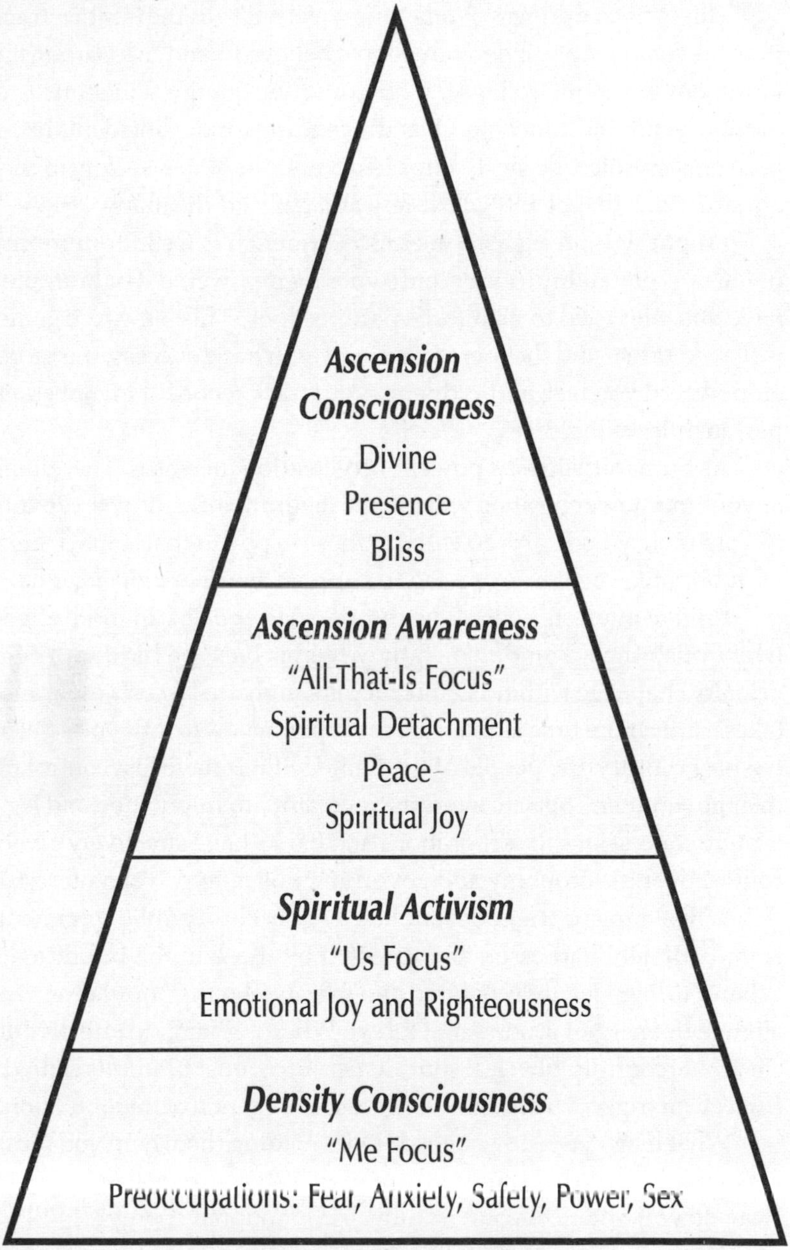
Ascension Consciousness
Divine
Presence
Bliss
Ascension Awareness
"All-That-Is Focus"
Spiritual Detachment
Peace
Spiritual Joy
Spiritual Activism
"Us Focus"
Emotional Joy and Righteousness
Density Consciousness
"Me Focus"
Preoccupations: Fear, Anxiety, Safety, Power, Sex

Pyramid of Spiritual Awakening

This is a basic principle sometimes referred to as the law of attraction. So, for example, if enough people believe in and focus upon an imminent economic collapse, their collective energy will stimulate events toward that outcome. Over the centuries, many incidents have been created solely because controlled fears stimulated society to create situations that benefited the few and harmed the many.

Prophecy is an exercise in empowerment. As we lift our vibrational rate, our ability to affect outcomes is empowered. For example, have you ever tried to manifest a parking spot? This New Age game is played often, and the more frequently you have success, the more empowered you feel, and suddenly your track record at manifesting parking places increases.

As humanity lifts, its power of co-creation increases. Therefore, anyone in a power position will use the media to influence perception toward their agenda. It is essential to those in power that some degree of public alignment is expressed to support their personal agenda.

Private interests behind the throne, so to speak, can more effectively push their agenda when they themselves are hidden. Their primary challenge within a democracy is simply that it costs more and takes a little more time as there are more politicians to influence. Over the past century, the people of the United States have lost control of their government. Special interests, regulatory manipulation and legislative concessions to corporations and banks have effectively given control over the economy and governing policy to private interests.

When a major trigger event like 9/11 occurs, public sentiment is immediately harnessed and directed by those in the public eye. When a foreign leader is painted as a threat, then the population can align their energies around that threat. When a solar flare knocks out electronic controls, physical control measures must be implemented. Each event triggers fear and also exposes the agenda of manipulation.

What magazines do you read? Does reading them help you form your opinions? What movies scare you? What stories inspire you? How do you organize your attitude and emotional energy?

These questions are important because they offer to you a deeper self-inquiry, a place to begin that relaxes the inner grip of control and opens up to the recognition that it is all a game. The experience of life is an opportunity to navigate power, control, creation of ideas, beliefs and experiences. Humans have organized those experiences into strata of approved experiences and beliefs. This is a paramount understanding, as many already know that "approved beliefs" are not necessarily truth. For countless centuries there was an approved belief that the world was flat. Contradicting this belief could endanger one's life until someone had the courage to break through the paradigm. Human history is filled with profound paradigm shifts.

When the heart comes forward and the ego relaxes, we remember that we are in a co-creative game in which the players have forgotten that they agreed to participate. There are steps one can take to release the grip of density consciousness upon you. It all begins with a willingness to surrender to the divine. In that surrender, one can start discovering the fear based strategies of the ego and recognizing the wisdom of the soul.

Consciousness is all you have—your sole possession. Everything else is secondary, and a distraction at that. Everything else is the game of you being in a body while having forgotten your true identity and origin. Divine wisdom infiltrates your life experience as you realign your consciousness with the "real you," your soul.

Self-Ascension is the process of reclaiming your true identity, of living authentically in alignment with that truth, while still having a body, a human experience. Only you are awake and no longer walking around in delusion.

Is that crazy? Some may think that it is. Crazy is the convenient way of throwing out anything that is too far away from the accepted paradigm or from your preferred way of being.

We are infinitely creative beings. As humans we have a tendency to take the path of least resistance. This predisposition has given rise to the commitment to prophecy and prediction, while simultaneously making fear and control so profitable that they seek to seed your consciousness to self-preserve.

This brings us to the recognition that our discernment is being invited to awaken through the game. When you anchor your clarity, your discernment comes forward, and the convergence of all wisdom and prophecy reveals itself to you.

As the Essene Brethren, (Ess-See-Nah energy[17]) have come forward again on our planet to share the lost books with us, this process reveals itself with true clarity.

FROM THE LOST BOOKS OF THE ESSENE, BOOK NINE: DISCERNED AWAKENED BEINGNESS:

Through the gift of discernment, the egoic filter will first offer to you the stamina of great tenacity. The egoic filter has great stamina. Often it has greater stamina than the physical body, which is why, when the egoic filter rises, the physical body may get tired.

Pay attention when you are in an interchange of ideas or interchange of energy or interchange of conversation. Do you feel energized, or do you feel depleted?

The egoic filter will always deplete because of the rich stamina it has, and the energy of beauteous discernment will always energize because it does not take.

It offers balance energy. Discernment is balance.

Offer to yourself now the following visualization.

Close your eyes, if you feel so called to do so, and as you close your eyes, as you allow yourself this gift, you call to mind an interchange that perhaps was not as comfortable as you would have wished it to be. Do not dwell on the specifics of the interchange. Simply dwell on how your body felt afterward.

Did you need to rest from the interchange?
Did you need to eat because of the interchange?
Did you need to go lay down because of the interchange?
Did you need to take a break because of the interchange?
Did you need to recuperate because of the interchange?

Then, indeed, the egoic filter was rearing the stamina of the ego, thereby finding its energetic pull from it, thereby literally depleting your energy.

This is not a judgment. It is the recognition of the great gift of discernment, because the great gift of discernment will illuminate all of the other practices we have offered to you.

As we mentioned, this is your present wrapped in beautiful paper and ribbon placed at your feet. If you wish to take advantage of this present, then open up your discernment and empower the stamina of discernment to energize, reenergize, sustain, revitalize, rejuvenate and continue the energetic stream around you with positive harmonic balance. This is discernment. Do you understand now? Yes.

And as you breathe again, take in a deep and beauteous breath.

As you can feel through this sharing from the Essene Brethren, when we allow ourselves to call forth our full discernment, we become more aligned with our true nature and less influenced by the game.

This brings us to the next energy that is a potential barrier to breaking free: attachment. As we are attached to the expected norms and paradigms of mass consciousness, while we may not always feel comfortable with them, we find it easy to stay aligned with them because of our attachments. It is nearly impossible to see the game for what it is while you are living with your attachments.

It is challenging to life to a new level of consciousness if you are attached to the traits of the current level. The following discourse offers a fresh perspective on this energy:

THE LOST BOOKS OF THE ESSENE, BOOK II: THE HEART OF ESSEENAH

We speak to you about the release of attachment because many of you seek Ascension. You seek keys of Ascension. You seek the energy of reconnecting to the ability to fly, which you have always had.

However, when you walk this planet without your EsSeeNah shoes, you walk seeking to be attached: to be attached to your life experience, to be attached to an outcome, to be attached to one way or another way, to be attached to a point of view that may be so important that you are unable to move forward. And this is okay.

What is it you are attached to?
What is it you are truly part of?
What attraction could there possibly be that would need to be called to you that is not already you?
You must listen for a moment to your own heart.
In your own heart and in your own soul and in your own energy field is everything you need.
Everything you need. Everything you need.

When the EsSeeNah walked your planet with great frequency and great regularity, many were afraid of EsSeeNah. Many projected energies toward EsSeeNah out of the fear of a mis-understanding what EsSeeNah is.

When you walk in Divine wholeness without needing to attach, without needing to call forth attraction, you walk and all is offered, all is given.
All doors and all windows are open.
All abundance that you could ever try to call forward for you is available, and oftentimes comes forward with such great waves of energy that you are, indeed, almost afraid of it.
Great waves of energy ... great waves of energy ...
great waves of energy.

How much energy do you spend reading about how to attract, learning how to attract, out-focusing on how to attract; paying attention to how you should attract; writing little sentences about how you should attract; talking to others about attracting; repeating your sentences?

When that energy is freed from your energy field, all there is, is the Divine perfection abundant being that you are.
That is the heart of EsSeeNah.

Transcending the prophecies / predictions and mainstream opinions is not an easy task, and yet it is one that you can master. It does take a sincere commitment to release the hypnosis of the density paradigm and here are seven steps to make that journey easier and more successful!

Seven steps to protect your evolutionary opportunity.

1. Recognize that freedom comes from within. No one will give you permission to ascend into your higher truth. Only you can give this gift to yourself.
2. Take action to align your choices with your highest truth. Stop pretending to be less than who you really are.
3. Compromise is death to your creativity. Never compromise your joy. If you are in a situation that seems to demand a compromise, step back, breathe and look deeper. Let your creativity find a way to honor the truth of your soul while offering respect to others' truth. You can do this while respecting all involved.
4. Unplug from density events, density environments, density foods and asleep people. The creations of density emit an energy that encourages you to fall asleep. If your best friends challenge who you are and make you feel less than that, are you ready to fully thank them for the gift of helping you know that it is time to move on?
5. Trust the invisible opportunity. There is only the now and the soon to be now…let the past go. Be present to what is alive in the moment and follow the joy.
6. Sing, tone, move and connect with the greater flow of creation. Art, conversation, music, writing, these are all open opportunities to relax into creation.
7. Smile and breathe deeply. There is only love. Beauty is everywhere. Be in joy.

Your Miracle Moment

This message is from the Ascended Master Jeshua[18]:

Greetings of love to thee! As my heart sits upon each mountaintop, my love surrounds all like the great oceans of your world of presence. The union of the heart and the love is an infinitely patient gift that silently and humbly awaits for all to open. With the opening of this gift comes the recognition that you are the master incarnate. May you know that you are filled with the spirit, love, presence and strength to BE the LIGHT of the DIVINE.

Is this not a miracle? Is this not the greatest gift ever found?

Often, my words are mistaken, so I offer few words, so that you are able to patiently and abundantly understand them, FEEL them, and KNOW that you are the infinite miracle of all that has ever been.

May each mountain bring you greater heart, and every ocean before you, a sea of love.

From the infinite depths of Oneness, I AM.

Chapter Four

ALLNESS FOLDING
INTO ONENESS

"BEFORE YOUR PLANET, BEFORE THIS REALM,
BEFORE THE FORM OF THE BODY THAT
YOU ARE IN RIGHT NOW, THERE WAS THE
DANCE OF DIVINE ONENESS."[19]

Communicating our Guatemalan journey has been challenging. The ability to fully express the energy, experience and power that we walk with during each moment we are there is not an easy task, yet, it is one that beckons us with greater and greater clarity each and every day.

How do you fully experience the profound opening of your galactic heart as the center of all divine remembrance? What do you feel when you gaze into the eyes of a Mayan high priest who serenely smiles as his eyes turn to liquid light? What happens to your human breath as you walk ancient forest trails in and breathe in light, love and eons of mastery?

Each of these questions come before us in rapid succession, over and over again. Often, as we are immersed in the quantum field, eternity of remembrance embraces us in what feels like a second, and then days of integration unfold around us. The dance with divine love is neither planned nor accidental, it simply is. Each of us, when in the moment of knowing, will either say yes or turn away. We chose to say yes.

We were back on the boat, and TOSA La Laguna in Guatemala was now in our sight. The day was perfect. The sun was shining, the leaves of the trees and the magnificent colors of the myriad of flowers all dazzling after the fresh rain. The smell of old growth forest is unmistakable and a rare treasure to be cherished. Arriving at the small lagoon, we stood on shore at the rocky landing dock as our eyes filled with tears of recognition that soon many would come to this land and experience the gift that we were receiving in this moment. The energy of appreciation was overwhelming.

Kira immediately lost all connection with this world and was quickly escorted to the Merkabah deck overlooking the lake. She kept muttering something about "they are here and waiting for us."

A small group of local Maya were interested in assisting with the preservation of this sacred land, and Sri Ram Kaa led them to the ancient trails within the forest high above the lake. As the party headed into the jungle, the lake glistened, and Kira Raa fell deep into connection with the many light beings who had come to share.

The Merkabah deck is quite extraordinary. Built on a firm foundation, it sits high above the lake and has endless views of the water, volcanoes, sky and shoreline. To sit in its center is truly a portal on the earth simply awaiting one who is present to activate its true purpose for being.

Holding the sacred, ancient artifact that had been gifted to her in Antigua, Kira simply allowed the spiraling energy that was consuming her to come into full presence. It was in this moment the immense crystalline pyramid above the lake revealed itself and the city of light appeared in full view.

Kira Raa communes with the lake on the Merkabah deck at TOSA La Laguna.

There are no words to offer you, only the invitation to gaze at the photo we have included and to be present with your own light and love. This city is no longer seeking to be hidden and will reveal itself to those who are ready to receive it in love, light and service.

The first words that we heard were, "There is great love and peace here. This is the heart of the heart."

The direct view from the center of the Merkabah deck into the city. Notice the "sleeping giant" mountain just to the right of the center—a powerful protector.

Many languages were speaking at once as Kira tried to simply be present for them all. Then she heard, "This is TOSA, and in Spanish, as it will be known here and from now on, it means, Tiene, Ocho, Suprema, Ascensión."

This literally translates as: Have Eight Supreme Ascension.

"What does this mean?" Kira asked quietly.

At that moment an ascended master who has asked to not be named yet appeared in full body and placed before Kira the heart of the heart. It was the Ascended Heart, intertwined with another Ascended Heart, opening a divine portal of connection. The two together had eight spokes, and the master smiled.

The master continued and said, "Muy presente y mystico 'gathering.'"

This literally translates as "A very present and mystical gathering."

As the tears of joy and recognition flowed steadily from Kira Raa, she was asked to simply be present for more information and to pick up her small video camera. Barely able to move, she listened and recorded a two-minute film to be shown at the behest of the Masters, "when those who are ready will understand."

Then the final message from the master was offered: "Be present to stillness, be active to know, serve awareness and be oneness . . . All is well."

For what had seemed like hours, Kira simply was present to this energy and blessing on behalf of the energies of our rapidly escalating world. Sri and his small group of Maya were present at the deck now simply witnessing this connection, and everyone shed abundant tears.

May we each know that the revelation of those abodes of the ascended masters that have long been hidden are now all coming forward out of great love and compassion for our world. May we each hold our divine love as a focus of presence as we recognize that within the energy of pure love, all interference energy dissipates!

※ ※ ※

Humanity is the expression of soul refractions and fractures exploring density. We have traveled far, and like a rubber band that has been stretched and stretched, it is time to relax back into oneness.

Moving in this direction calls forth the great recognitions, and this sharing from the Essene Brethren fully discloses the energies we are working with and our choices for how we greet them.

FROM THE LOST BOOKS OF THE ESSENE: BOOK FIVE

The Essene Brethren Speak:

It is the time to come forward in the energy of Divine upliftment in the time of great beauty…great beauty, for many have held out or have let go of the gift of beauty.

Embracing Beauty

What is beauty? What is it to truly understand beauty…to be beautiful…to be filled with the understanding and the recognition of the Divine beauty that exists in all and in all-ness?

We especially wish to understand the beauty of Allness, and, indeed, this is a powerful lesson, because Oneness is not a concept. Oneness is not a little thing you write down and make a little diagram of.

Oneness is the reunion of the precious gift, and the understanding, and the integration, of all beauty...Of all beauty.

And yet, in a world of words, as your world is a world of words, when you hear the word beauty, you already have a thought with it; do you not? Yes. As with each word, you have a thought.

When we offer you the word Oneness, you have a thought. When we offer you Allness, you have a thought.

To be thought-less is to find true beauty.

*To be thought-less is to be able to find true beauty. Now, you may say to be thoughtless in our world, that is to be selfish. We say to be thought-less...**Less thought!***

There is a great and powerful momentum that is part of your own evolutionary Divine upliftment that has come forward now like a great and profound beautiful lion gracefully exiting the forest. Coming forward to say, I am here. I have grown up. Do you see my beauty?

The Lion Leaves the Woods

As the lion comes out of the forest for all to see, it offers two energies immediately: The energy of divine empowerment — I am safe to come out of the woods, I am safe to be seen in my power — and the energy also that says, I am here from the energy of Divine empowerment, and it is my heart that I offer as the goal of your heart.

Now, we wish to explain this.

When a lion comes out of the woods, it is a courageous act indeed, is it not? This is because for a lion to come out of its woods means it is to expose itself, to be seen. It must be in great power to do this because it knows when it comes out of the safety of its den or its home into full daylight, that it is now offering itself to all of the energies that are prepared to greet it.

The Energies that Greet Us

Each energy carries with it a different intent; does it not?

There is the energy of the one who says, I will receive this gift. I will see the beauty of this gift and I will not run away. I wish to run up and pet the lion because I can see the Oneness I am with the lion, and the lion understands this energy and sits gently, saying, Pet me, and I shall offer you my love in return.

And then there is the energy of the one who has sat in their own woods hidden so that when the lion comes out, they can catch it by surprise, hunt it, take it as the prize that it is.

In the hunted energy of the lion, the lion has no fear because it has known that the hunter has waited. And so the lion does not shrink from that fear. And if, indeed, the energy of the lion is meant to become one with the hunter, then the lion transcends and understands this, too.

*And then there are those who are afraid of the lion, who run the other way. A lion! Oh, my goodness. I must run away. The lion will eat me; it will scratch me; it will hurt me. And so the lion sits and simply watches them run without the need to chase...**without the need to chase.***

You see, Beloved Ones, you are at the great powerful moment
where the time of In-lion-ment is in full energetic flow —
full energetic flow — and you are either a cub or an adult.

Which do you seek to be, and how do you seek to offer this gift?

Seeking Understanding

And you say now, how does this become a book of the Essene? Let us offer you the understanding that is deeper.

To understand and to come out of the woods,
can only happen after you have prepared yourself
through your own self-understanding and presence
and release of all doubt that has held you
in many different journeys.

To sit quietly at the edge of a woods to be seen by all is a gift of mastery, because the lion does not come out and let out a roar. The lion walks out and says, I am here, through its presence. And through great presence you find beauty.

Through great presence you find beauty.

In your world, how many times have you looked at something that someone says, Oh, that is so funny looking! It could be a tree, it could be a puppy or a little dog or a person or a building, and yet in your own heart you find beauty because it is standing with presence; because it is aware; because it says, I am here, and I am aware.

To be aware is to find the beauty within and the beauty in all.

Beauty is a seed of the soul that has come forward for you now in a world that has sought to disrupt it, freeze it, characterize it, minimize it, and gather it into a disrupted manipulated face.

The Pristine Seed of your Heart
Beauty, Beloved Ones, begins in the pristine energy of your heart center.

Deep in your heart center is pristine energy. Think of the clearest mountain lake that you have ever seen. As you drink of that water, how does it feel? When you simply see that lake, what do you experience? Just arriving at the lake, do you smile? Do you simply sit in awe and say or feel, What beauty! What a gift!

This beauty, this gift, is the pristine seed of your own heart, and yet, do you awaken that seed or do you pollute the lake, because the choice is yours; is it not?

If you go to a beautiful lake, do you ever find a cup thrown by the side, or do you find the cup that is full? What do you do with it? This is an important understanding.

You must find beauty in all experience and action in order to be able to swim in the pristine energy of your heart.

To swim in the pristine energy of your heart will bring consistent and fulfilling nourishment to the body, to the mind, to the soul, to the spirit, and you will find that you no longer require so much sleep.

You will find that you do not require so much stimulation from external sources. You will find that deep within the Divine Presence of this lake of your heart is all of the restoration, abundance, nourishment, love, connection and beauty you could ever want, and yet to want implies there is an unmet need.

And so we come again to share to be thought-less is to discover beauty.

To be thought-less is to discover beauty.
The planetary cosmic connection is a powerful one when you seek mastery and when you seek the release of hiding in the woods.
Until you can free yourself to be thought-less and to engage in the cosmic ocean, then you are in the woods and the woods is indeed beautiful; is it not?
It can be quite lovely. And so allow that to be.

The Mastery Virus

Perhaps the day has come when you have found a path that will take you to the edge of the forest. This is a great gift. And, you can always camp along the way, if you need to.

When you are ready, this gift of beauty will propel you out of the woods because there is no longer anything to hide.

And when you come forward, you come forward as a lion. As you come forward as a lion, you are prepared, because you know there are three potential energies waiting for you:
1. The energy of the embrace,
2. The energy of the hunter, and
3. The energy of the one who is afraid.
All greet you with one of these three energies, Beloved Ones. Simply, are you greeted in the woods or not? If you are greeted in the woods with

these energies, then you are greeting each other at a level that has not yet mastered beauty.

It is the time of great practice for this, is it not?

For most of your planet is very much in the woods. Some are closer to the edge than others, yet, indeed, there are big cats in the woods right now, and this is good.

How are you greeted and when you are greeted,
and the opportunity to be a lion in the greeting,
is the gift of mastery that comes through the recognition
that you are now connecting with a cosmic consciousness freeing
the cerebrum from the doldrums of density.

Recognizing the Three Energies
When you decide, and it is a decision that you make,
and it is not a decision that can go two ways,
so when you make the decision to embrace mastery,
to celebrate mastery, and to move forward with mastery,
you will face all three of the energies of the lion.

You will face those who run to you and say, Let me hold you. Let me gaze into your eyes. Let me acknowledge you. Spend as much time as you can with those who have no reason to treat you otherwise.

And you will greet those who say, Let me hunt you. I wish for you to not even exist in this form. And there are many ways they will do this.

In your world, a very acceptable way to hunt you is with words. Words are very good at stopping you from being who you are, if you let them. They are the tool of the hunter in a world of density who seeks to stop a lion who has found their power.

Words mean nothing unless you are trapped in the thought of density. If you are, and you have this experience, and you start feeling less than, then this, too, is part of your path of mastery. You have met the energy and you are aware and you get to practice again. Sometimes a retreat back into the woods can be rejuvenating; can it not? Yes.

ALLNESS FOLDING INTO ONENESS

Then there are those who will seek to run away from you, and of course it will be your fault! This is important to understand because if they are running, and you must understand people who run, even animals who run... run for one reason: **They are afraid!**

An animal that runs from another animal only runs because it is afraid, and it is afraid at a cellular level it does not even understand. It just knows it must run away.

If you are a little mouse and you see a hawk in the sky, you run away. If you are an empowered Being of Light on a planet, standing out of the woods in your power and there are those around you who cannot experience that power, then they will run away because they are afraid.

The beauty in this gift is that you can send them reassurance with your energy propelled from your heart. This will then ignite your heart to even greater mastery and even more extraordinary presence, manifest abundance, and Divine understanding.

Or... you can choose to engage in the run, which is usually very exhausting; is it not?

Beloved Ones, this teaching is very important to understand. To come out of the woods and to see the beauty in all is a freedom that can only be called in to you by you. Only you know.

The Blessing of the Three Energies: True Soul Nourishment
When you find the beauty in all of these experiences . . .
when you find that the beauty exists in the endless,
divine, pristine lake that is within your heart . . .
when you dive into this ocean because, indeed, it is an ocean,
and an endless one at that, often and regularly . . .
what you will find is that you
will no longer succumb to being tired, overwhelmed, depressed,
scared, worried, or have a lack of affluence.

There are so many words we could offer you that come from a thought pool that is doing its best to perpetuate the energy to keep you in the woods.

Now, Beloved Ones, there is a co-creative state that will propagate this energy very quickly, and so we wish for you to hear this: How do you nourish your bodies?

Do you eat fear, or do you eat light?
Do you eat love, or do you eat death?
Do you drink water that is pure and crystalline and clear,
or do you drink bubbles that irritate your stomach?
Choices, Beloved Ones.

Start with these choices. Gaze at your food. Lift it up in the hand and hold it like you would a baby and say, Look how beautiful you are! Thank you. Thank you. Thank You, for offering me this gift in this moment right now, and slowly ingest with love and joy, patience.

You have teeth for one reason, to liquefy your food. You are predominantly water. If you do not liquefy your food, you are putting hard matter into a water substance. Like a rock thrown into a pond, it is heavy and it sinks.

Chew your food, and with each bite perhaps you say, "Thank you. I love you." Chew. Thank you. Chew. I love you. Chew. Thank you. Chew. I love you. Chew. Thank you. Chew. I love you. Chew until all that is left is water and then the water can lovingly assimilate into a body without any—without any—discomfort.

If your nourishment brings your body discomfort,
then there is not enough love in the nourishment.
It is that simple. It is that simple.

As you slowly chew your food, we encourage you also to know that your bodies were never meant to drive and eat. A wondrous concept of a density based world, one hand with a sandwich and one hand with a wheel.

Your bodies were never designed for this. When you had horses, it was physically impossible—and yet you would try. We simply wish for you to understand that when your life was made transportation-friendly so that you could see more people more frequently and more quickly, it was not so you could eat along the way.

Perhaps if you need to eat along the way, you can eat the nourishment of the Divine.

Move your mouth in sacred mantra. Sing to beautiful music. Uplift your heart and your soul and rejuvenate.
If you need to do something with the mouth, then drink water, and you will find that you will arrive uplifted, your body will feel light and fresh, your energy field delightful, and that beautiful pristine lake in your heart is overflowing with extraordinary energy. We simply wish for you to consider this.

Your world has, indeed, moved faster now; has it not?

Your body seeks stillness in a fast world.
When you eat fast, you de-program your bliss.

When you shove food down your throat, when you allow yourself to starve, you are truly saying, I have not had enough water today.

If you carry with you water all the time, the Water of Life, all the time, you will never go hungry, ever. If you breathe the Breath of Life with a smile and connect it into your heart, you will never feel a loss. And if you chew your food with Thank you, I love you, you will find great joy and bliss in what you eat, and you will find that perhaps your body has had more than it needed all along and has not known what to do with the waste product.

Beloved Ones, beauty begins when you honor the vessel that you have brought forward to hold your soul to express on this planet.

Love your body. Keep it clean, and cleanliness is more than taking shower or bath. It begins with the inside nourishment. Keep your body clean and allow your joy to come forward, your beautiful lake of Divine Presence. And then, Beloved Ones, the hair of the lion is silky and beautiful and fragrant, the eyes are clear, the muscles strong, the bones beautiful. The cells harmonize each other, the blood glows, the heart pumps, and you step out of the woods and say, I am here, and I am ready, and nothing can interfere with my Divine Presence. And I meet your Divine Presence with my Divine Presence in beauty, harmony, synergy and understanding.

Beloved Ones, we will take a few questions. Yes?

"I have two children, a 17-year-old and a 13-year-old, and their energy is very strong. The example that you're giving us with the lion that is being strong and coming out of the woods, I think I've been standing right by the edge scared to death to go outside, feeling like the fool to be out there. And sometimes I wonder if I go through that change as a mother, is that going to be enough of an example for my kids? They're my practice, because they're wanting to do their thing, eat their food, and think their way. And they look at me, you know, with feeling like they have the power and they have the right to choose what they're choosing. I've taught them that, and I know it's true, and at the same time I feel maybe I taught them wrong."

So breathe first. We wish for you to understand that your question is asked by many and for many reasons. Every parent in the world of Gaia, every parent, not one is excluded, has the opportunity to free their children by their own example.

This means your children will not respond to your words. They will only respond to your consistent action. When you hide, you teach them to hide. When you are afraid, you teach them to be afraid.

In your world, each child, as you know, selects the extraordinary parents that bring them forward. Therefore, you cannot have taught them wrong. You must hear this. That is the mind of density that would believe you could have taught them wrong, and a wonderful step along your path of mastery.

Their strength is offering you a mirror of how strong you are, and you must stand in your own clarity and your own power to free them to have their own. This is why in many families there is a belief in cycles of diseases. One mother has a cancer, then the daughter has the cancer, then the grand-daughter has the cancer.

This is not a gene. It is an energy.

To be the one who stands and declares, I will break the cycle, has not been openly supported in your world, and so it is very hard.

Oftentimes, when you stand in your power, children rebel like 2-year-olds—tantrum, tantrum…tantrum. It is important to hold your power in the tantrum. And sometimes, even separation comes forward in your world, and even then you must hold Inner Presence.

We are offering this in many terms for you and for all those who ask this question.

To be a parent is to love enough to let the child have their life while you do not compromise your own.

In your world, especially in the role of mother which has been greatly out of balance in your planet now for many hundreds of years, the role of mother has too commonly become the role of enabler in your world, a role of self-sacrifice that thereby perpetuates this gift which can be a gift to the children who then become enablers who then perpetuate the gift.

You are at a moment of great freedom because you are aware.

Yes, it takes great strength to do this, and this is the gift of the three energies we speak of today. When you become the lion and step out of the woods, you must remember the first energy we mentioned.

There have been those who have been waiting to come hold you. There are those who have been waiting to support you. But they are out of the woods, and unless you come out of the woods, they cannot join you because they are free of the woods. Remember that this is the first energy…the ones who will run to you, understand your journey and stand by your side because they are out of the woods, too.

If one who is in the woods seeks to help you get out of the woods when they are still in the woods themselves, you will never break through.

And we are complete.

Beloved Ones, welcome out of the woods.

Your Miracle Moment

This Message is from the Crystalline Brethren of the Angels of Light:

> Beloved ones of the planet earth we sing to thee the harmonies of the universe. We come to you as a union of all the energies you know and experience as the Angelic realms. We offer to you simply the energy and expansion of light and love when recognized as the union of all experienced as The One.

> Deep within the core centers of your beloved bodies are the energies of one love, one light and one experience. Through your manifestation as vessels of energy that contain the experience of all, the calling forth of your essential harmony of union is bringing you closer to your reunified self as the forefront of your every expression.

> May our core center express itself with sound as your heart calls it forth without any hesitancy…may your soul's voice be heard. As you loosen all tightness that surrounds your core center, the release of joyful energy illuminates your presence and your essential harmony of the unified light will express with ever greater presence, ever greater joy and the gift of creation in the form of abundant co-creative expression of love.

> As we sing to thee we hear the voice of your soul, the song of love, the harmony of all life. May your song be heard by your vessel of the earth as well, and may you find great joy in claiming your essential co-creative harmony now. With great love we invite you to close your eyes and hear us now.

Chapter Five

THE END OF THE
PEOPLE OF MAIZE

"WHEN ONE IS FOCUSED ON THE NEED TO
RELIEVE PAIN IN ANY WAY, THEN ONE UNABLE TO
FOCUS ON THE NOURISHMENT OF LOVE."[20]

Learning how the Maya feel and respond is a great challenge to one who is not indigenous. Many well-intended transplants from other countries who have a myriad of tales to tell and warnings to offer. "You'll never understand them" is a common warning, along with the other frequently chanted mantra, "They will never accept you."

We have learned that you can depend on two things when learning how to interface with the Maya who are living their lives, raising families and doing their best to earn a living: they will always say yes to anything, even when they have absolutely no intention of following through, and they have the most amazing smiles that come forth genuinely and frequently.

To witness a culture that has rarely intermarried throughout the generations is to be literally staring at an ancient race in its pure form. Most Maya are not much taller than five feet and have a strong facial structure that exudes pride, knowledge, hard work and the challenges of being constantly invaded over many centuries.

The high priests carry the open energy, the energy that sees beyond one village and one way of being. Yet many of them will not share this with any of their village because they know that most would not understand. Young Maya also share the dilemma faced by modern-day young Tibetans, the lack of connection to their heritage and the desire among the youth to gravitate toward the ways of the developed world, without recognizing the need to keep their rich heritage alive.

There are many wonderful books you can read to understand the history of the Maya, however we wish to share you with the energy of the Maya of today and how it translates into our greater awakening. For within the perceived simplicity is a great lesson, and we discover with each journey that the lessons just keep pouring forth.

On a sunny Saturday in the sleepy village of San Antonio Palopó, Kira Raa sat down with a local Maya woman named Mariana. She was eager to offer her assistance to Kira and to the TOSA students who would be arriving in a few days. She also wanted to demonstrate her ability to interface with international visitors.

Mariana was a typical villager in many respects and yet she and her husband had "real world" experience since they had actually left the village for awhile and lived in Antigua, the city of walls, where they worked at a hotel briefly. Mariana's family, like most, needed extra income and there was very little opportunity for work in the village.

Sitting with Mariana was quite an adventure. The eagerness and the smiles were so forthcoming, yet the constant yeses were concerning. Her job would be to prepare meals for ten people twice a day for seven days and to prepare them according to Soul Nourishment[21] guidelines. As with all meetings in the village, this one was already going into the third hour without yet discussing details.

Finally, after Mariana had a good concept of what Soul Nourishment was, Kira asked what seemed like a simple question. "Mariana, what would you like to cook? What type of lunches and dinners would you suggest?"

The question brought forward a look of terror and confusion across her face that was startling. What had happened? The buoyant, smiling local villager suddenly looked out of place and confused. We were seeing in action the safety that many experience in being told what to do. Mariana needed boundaries and guidelines. She needed a sense of confidence that she would only find in the familiar.

Fully aware of the experience that was unfolding, Kira quickly started writing down meals on a day-to-day basis, and Mariana became buoyant and participative again. The meals were not a completely new concept, as they were loosely based upon her traditional cooking. However there would be no live chickens being purchased at a market for the evening meal, and there was an introduction of tofu, a new food to Mariana.

Kira carefully pulled the tofu out of the refrigerator and Mariana instantly said, "*¿Queso?*" (Cheese?)

Mariana and her daughter prepare a blessing ceremony
before an evening meal at TOSA La Laguna.

Kira smiled and proceeded to explain that this was a substitute for her *pollo* (chicken). Mariana watched tentatively as Kira sliced, chopped, crumbled and prepared the tofu in all the ways Mariana would cook her chicken, and all seemed well.

A week later, as Mariana was happily cooking a meal with the very happy assistance of her young daughter, Kira realized that it was not one of the meals from the menu they had created during their five-hour marathon meeting. Upon further questioning the guests, it turned out that Mariana was happily making her handmade corn tortillas, black beans and assorted vegetables without any chicken, and the guests were so happy with the food that not one knew anything was amiss.

After the guests left, Kira also discovered all the fresh tofu shoved into the back of the refrigerator, shriveled, molded and sadly neglected.

What had happened? Everything was set, the meals had been planned and Mariana had been prepared.

The greater lesson unfolding was that Mariana was demonstrating the energy prevalent in all of humanity. Through her lack of "sophisticated" interaction, she was demonstrating a truth that many hide, yet still act out.

She was comfortable with her way of cooking. She knew how to prepare her dishes in her way. And despite her sincere desire to learn a new way, it was easier to stay with the known and receive approval, rather than venture into the unknown and risk mistakes along the way.

Humanity, too, is collectively at this great point. Many are crying out with sincere desire to shift energy on the planet. Many claim to be awakening and wanting a positive future. Yet, the vast majority are simply more comfortable complaining about what they see around them than walking through the discomfort of taking action.

The Mayan high priests refer to this moment as the End of the People of Maize. Corn is the ethereal currency of the Maya. It is the material substance that offers health and wealth through its cultivation. Its very presence is life.

As we gaze on our world of creation, without clinging to denial, we can see that humanity as a collective has been on a chosen a path of great pain. In a mere 200 years we have destroyed the rain forests, polluted our waters and atmosphere, supported a norm of lowering school standards and allowed profit-motivated corporations to make decisions concerning our natural resources, food supply and health care.

Our natural resources are "owned" by corporations, and our ecosystem is damaged beyond any near-term repair. The public water is unfit for drinking and the air overhead is sprayed with unidentified chemicals and pesticides. Denial and ignorance have become the accepted norm.

Our world is potentially headed toward a violent transition phase simply because of an unwillingness to awaken. Conformity to the denial is a way of keeping the ego comfortable. Short-term thinking interrupts true responsibility.

We are immortal souls with an available connection to divine wisdom and the healing energy of divine love. We are immortal and we can cycle round and round the wheel of suffering for as long as we choose. The absolute truth is that the insanity will stop the moment we say "enough."

How much pain is enough? The slumbering masses will ultimately wait for the violent wake-up call. As children, most of us were predisposed to believe in powerful outside authorities, often a rescuer or wise king or queen. Those who sleep in density will rally around perceived rescuers and vote for new "kings." They do not know any better. As Mariana demonstrated with her reaction to Kira, most people inherently want to be led. They want boundaries.

They also do not read books like this. You, beloved readers, are the ones who often wrestle with your own drowsiness. You feel the Joy of your divine heart, and you also feel the compulsion to navigate your commitments with those in density. You dance between true freedom and obligation. Compromise is always present, and the pain of this can feed your capacity for denial.

Your time for action is now. As the world at large compresses into further density, the actions that are coming from the mainstream will seem insane to you. Earth changes, war, fuel shortages or acts of terrorism are certain to dance on center stage. Will you allow these storms to dictate your joy?

To grow into full awakening means surrendering all need to control. True growth always feels uncomfortable at first. There is no religion, no secret herb, no meditation technique that will liberate you.

All the time-honored teachings offer one fact: the sincere student, the one who surrenders their ego's need to control, is the one who makes progress. It is not the meditation technique or spiritual practice that saves you. It is your sincerity.

It is your choice to surrender into the truth of your authentic being that propels you. Awakening does not happen because of a spiritual practice; it is the awakened consciousness within you that chooses the practice. You are already awake. You need only choose to cleanse the debris of slumber from your energy field.

As we come to the close of the People of Maize, the universe is rapidly handing out lessons and they are getting greater and clearer with each passing day.

To be present at the culmination of one cycle and the embarkation of another is a momentous moment. Everything that is clinging to the old structure will do its best to self-preserve, and the inevitable new cycle will be born. Will you let go of the old ways and lift into the new? This moment brings forward one primary message for all of humanity:

You must be clear what you want and willing to stay focused and committed to it.

Our planet is actively and diligently offering us messages everyday that she needs our clarity and our support. This loving gift from our beloved Gaia begs one important question of self-inquiry: "How can we offer to our planet that which we may not be sure we can offer to ourselves?"

While sitting with the 12 lessons from the *Lost Books of the Essene*, gifted through Kira in conjunction with the archangelic realm, we humbly recognize it is an imperative moment to not hold back in any way that which must be shared, regardless of public or private consequences. This is the time when truth, integrity and passionate action are called for.

Often, when we arrive at that divine moment of crystalline clarity, the support systems of our traditional life and experience of life may feel threatened. This is a normal experience. Yet it is an experience that can divert you from a focused pathway.

Must we come to the brink of our own destruction before we choose to shift from a life that destroys to a life that creates?

The moment of the End of the People of Maize is upon us.
Are you willing to let the attachment to materiality end?
Do you want to be ready?
Are you sure?

Then, beloved ones, it is time to *focus*. Fear is a regressive energy that collapses your power.

Try to break the loop that makes fear profitable. Allow yourself to fully embrace positive and passionate action vs. anger-based activism. We are at a very important moment in our collective history. Pick something, anything that your heart can believe in, and feel as real, *then be sure so stick with it.*

Many have written us lately with stories of being pulled off balance by well-intended teachers, authors and healers, and some of these are very well known. Remember that only you know what is right for you.

Denial is a universal aspect of human ego. We all deny and discard information that is too overwhelming or too challenging to our personal stability. On the personal level, for example, we deny that our poor eating habits will result in ill health. Whether we demand oxygen bottles, insulin shots and scooters instead of taking time away from our television shows to exercise and eat healthy nourishing foods, or simply rationalize that there is no time to cook a balanced meal, denial touches everyone in the mainstream.

We are also lax in allowing pharmaceutical corporations to define health and safety, while trusting a flu shot more than our own ability to manifest health. Strong immune function is a gift of living lives of greater harmony and less stress. While many are awake to this on an intellectual level, the reality is that when it comes to the personal experience, authority is given to the system in lieu of the trust of the self.

As part of our experience of density, at some point we have collectively denied our empowerment as sovereign, whole and healthy beings. The only possible way to step out of the denial is to gift yourself with the first big step: unplug from density consciousness.

The first step has become ever more challenging in a world of dependency-oriented marketing and coexistence. Yet, to unplug from your technological dependency upon outer resources, outside authorities, outside newscasters and all compromising relationships is the springboard to extraordinary personal freedom and abundant living.

In a recent communication from the T-12,[22] they shared the following:

> "You beloved ones are seeking greater balance and restoration. In the experience of density now, in your world now, many cry out and seek outside assistance to regain their balance. They seek outside information, outside affirmation, outside medication, outside illumination, all outer focused.
>
> And when you gaze into the solar flare of your own heart, you find the restoration of this harmony. And yet, beloved ones, in a world of mechanical machination, they expect, they offer, they invite, they induce, they encourage you to come deeper into the veil, deeper into the veil, deeper into the veil, deeper into the veil.
>
> What veil is it? And how did that veil come forward?
>
> The veil is the collective experience of the energy that is released in the sloughing of all negativity that is brought forward into a planetary thought body thereby pressing upon you at all times.
>
> It is enhanced, indeed fed by mechanical energies, electronic energies; and so it is richly fed. It is quite fat, is it not? It is very richly fed,

and many meals a day. Consistent meals, and a never-ending appetite to have more, have more, have more, so that more can feed back.

It is a cycle that once entered into cannot be removed from without the restoration of natural harmony, balance and soul restoral, as found within the gift of this divine planet of experience through the sun, through the moon, through the breath, through the light, through the understanding that ALL mechanical energy is a servant...all.

Beloved Ones, are you a slave to what you would call your mechanical servants?

Do you wake up to your email?

Do you go to bed checking your email?

Is your relationship with your email greater than your relationship with your heart, with your sun, with your moon?

Do you spend as much time with your sun, with your moon, with your heart, with yourself, as you do with your electronic interactions?

Do you paste electronic interactions to your ear so that you may share electronically as quickly as possible?

Do you punch little letters into a computer or a mini computer so that you may stay in contact so quickly, never allowing the stillness to be?

Beloved Ones, in your world now, there are the great resurrection energies igniting. The great resurrection energies are igniting from eons ago. Relax into this and you will have a greater presence of that which is coming forward."

Yes, it takes courage to unplug.

True freedom is an inner commitment to set yourself first. For many people it involves a deep cleansing, or shamanic death, of our previous way of being as these old ways have defined us and become our means of creating safety, however illusionary.

The shamanic death, part of the deepest unplugging, refers to the death of the ego. However, you can unplug from the unhealthy patterns and social groups without doing a battle to the death with your ego. It requires educating yourself and letting go of limiting beliefs. It requires a willingness to let go of false security and discover that *you* are the authority in your life who can summon incredible spiritual power by calling in your spiritual resources.

For now, we simply wish to connect you to the depth of denial that may be at work in your life experience. Denial is a form of prison. It keeps you disconnected from your true strength by empowering a limited sense of self that is unwilling to face fear.

It is time to honestly ask yourself: Am I ready to be free?

True freedom only comes when our love of truth and our trust in our own spiritual nature is greater than our fear.

If you have been blessed to witness anyone walk through fear, or if you have walked through your own, that magic moment unfolds when there is inherent trust and inner essence, even though that essence may defy description. It's the sense that "I just knew that I could get through it, even though I feared I would die, I knew I wouldn't, and here I am to talk about it now."

The moment of divine universal support is available to you now in ways that it has not been before. Are you ready to move into your greatest freedom by unplugging from the illusion and taking charge of your life? Perhaps the phrase "If not now, when?" has greater meaning in this moment than ever before!

What about our shared outer world? Each and every day many dismiss confronting the serious challenges in our world and the lies, often believed to be in our best interest, that are propagated by the power brokers of our modern society. The corruption runs as deep as the core of our existence. Profit agendas have infiltrated every aspect of society and created a norm that is disconnected from wholeness and healthy balance.

Whether it is allowing soda pop and snack foods into our elementary schools or standing by while armed forces interfere in the social and political development of other countries, we have allowed those who seek power and profit to manipulate our perspectives and corrupt public policy.

If you are ready to call forth self-honesty, you will discover that the United States is no longer the pinnacle of personal liberty, health and quality education. Many have looked the other way while corporations ravage our natural resources. We want to believe that technology will rescue us from the destruction of the biosphere. However, along with the economy, the world structures as we have known them are declining very rapidly. If you allow yourself the role of the observer, what you discover is that there no longer exists a true democracy in the U.S., only enough window dressing to keep the masses quiet and in denial.

Even the champion of hope, Barack Obama, has renewed the provisions of the Patriot Act, which would have given back some personal liberties to the American people. This only brings to light that Obama, like most modern politicians, was forced to comply. He had only one choice—to sell his ability to act in full integrity to the hidden power brokers who profit from the current levels of corruption.

Terrorism is a false enemy. It is a war that is impossible to win. Investing in schools, health care, farms and factories in other countries builds trust and interdependency. Instead we spend billions on troops, bombs and flawed military strategy that puts billions of dollars into private hands and creates a scenario in those countries that will insure conflict for many generations.

Conflict is more profitable than peace to those who choose to pull the strings of any society. Ironically, peace would produce far more economic growth, through the building of social, educational and medical infrastructures. However, those investments would not be as centralized as the war machine.

We are not politically motivated and have no agenda to promote in these pages other than: "Wake up!" It's not about being angry at your government, though many could focus on the bad faith and manipulation and feel outraged. It's not about picketing your bank, mortgage company, workplace or local hospital, although most of these institutions have placed short-term profit above global harmony, true compassion and sustainability.

These institutions are merely an honest reflection of our mass denial. We co-created this situation. And, if we don't immediately reprioritize our energy and attention, then World War III is a certainty. There are those deep within density that look forward to the conflict and have a subconscious fascination with the notion that a great war in the Middle East will trigger the return of a savior.

The denial inherent in such myths runs deep in the human psyche. And human beings tend to re-injure themselves in a tragic attempt to heal unconscious trauma. We are at the most important collective moment ever. What do you want it to look like?

We are co-creating an outcome based upon our level of consciousness. The world is a reflection of our inner state. To try to fix anything in the outer world without first healing the inner world is ineffective.

In our prior incarnation, Su'Laria,[23] we co-created planetary destruction. And whether you remember or believe that story, you will likely agree that deep in your own psyche is a sense that global catastrophe is likely. We seem to know that something terrible can occur, and we'd rather just place our attention elsewhere, or simply believe that somehow, magically, we won't be affected—that it will happen "somewhere else." The recognition deep inside is denied, and the energy expressed as fear and reactivity.

In global denial our earth's peoples will likely further polarize, unwittingly supporting a series of wars fueled by fundamentalists and experiencing earth changes that will rock the Northern and Southern Hemispheres. Death and destruction unlike anything witnessed in our recorded history may possibly wait just a few years ahead *unless* we shift our consciousness. Sometimes a crisis is the very thing needed to bring us to our senses.

The time of the completion of the People of Maize is at hand. How we bring about that completion is the single most important focus we have ever had. As we shift from the outer materialistic focus toward the essential, we begin to stabilize our hearts. Peace and patience flow more naturally.

Imagine how the various governments of the world will respond to ocean water levels rising 20 to 40 feet? Do we have the resources to move whole cities? Do we have health organizations that can offer any true solutions? Presently, we don't. The only thing we can offer is martial law. Is that really the option we want to bring forward?

The ice caps are melting far faster than predicted. Volcanic activity on the ocean floor will certainly generate more tsunamis. Yet our governments still want to invest heavily in armament, so they divert our attention by arguing about the truth and solutions of global warming, argue about the need to continue manufacturing land mines, and condone the continued dumping of city waste off barges onto the ocean floor.

We are at the moment where we are being invited to fully break free of all illusions and face the revealing self-truth: in the end, it will not be an environmental crisis that will cause our destruction. It will not be a planet colliding with the earth, nor will it be the fault of any government. In the end, we will come to once again realize that it is our co-creative choice to live in denial, to refuse to dissolve fear and instead distract ourselves from the essential that will manifest as our self-destruction—*if we choose.*

- What if you knew the world was going to end next month (or any specific date)?
- How would you live between now and then?
- Would you still do things that dulled your joy?
- Would you compromise your freedom?

We live each day with spirit blessing us by literally keeping our expansion on a "need-to-know basis." Tongue-in-cheek, perhaps, but if we all knew the hour and day of our earthly departure, would we learn as much? Would we embrace as much?

The truth is that if you knew for certain it all would come to an end in one month's time, chances are you would do the things that were truly important to you. Would you try to make peace with your emotions and your family? Would you still compromise? In the end, deep within your heart and spirit, a great recognition of divine experience would awaken inside. You might even celebrate a little!

More than ever, the sacred intention of the work of Self-Ascension shines in this critical moment of human history: to listen, to love and to hold the space of enlightenment for all.

As we carry forward the sacred intention of Self-Ascension in Guatemala and New Mexico, we celebrate many ceremonies on behalf of the energy of our world and the times just ahead. It is a gift to recognize the culmination of one way of living. After all, humanity has existed as the people of maize for a very long time. Perhaps we are ready to embrace our future with love and reverence instead of fear and hesitancy. Most importantly, perhaps we are ready to accept ourselves, our individuality, our commonality and our contributions. Consciousness emits a vibration that sends a wave into the planetary field. Are you vibrating at the levels of peace, love and joy? Or, do you add fear to the planetary thought body? May you fully recognize the importance of your role in the years ahead and our collective future together.

Your Miracle Moment

This Message is from the Beloved Ascended Master St. Germaine:
*Dearest ones of wondrous and luminous light and love!
We beseech thee now to claim the birthright of your divine heritage as beings of fullness bestowed with the brilliance and magnificence of all light and love.*

Your ability to bring presence to this world is the gift of the universe that opens the doors of divine remembrance for all. Begin with yourself! Release any doubt that you are the divine in action, at all times. As you allow yourself to be fully embraced by this action of knowing and loving, you are then the instantaneous manifestation of all that is, in all ways.

Ask yourself now: 'What inside of this wonderful body would ever seek to deny the truth of my magnificence?'

As you walk with presence every moment of every day may you bring your attention to this question until the full presence of your knowing brings a smile of divine recognition to your face and ALL aligns to support your journey. Beloved ones, the time is upon you. Gift yourself with knowing beyond all doubt, and simply be present for the unfoldment of yourself!

Chapter Six

THE BEGINNING OF THE PEOPLE OF HONEY

"YOUR WORLD IS MEANT TO OFFER YOUR
GREAT SUPPORT. FREE YOURSELF TO
RECEIVE IT, AND IT IS UNLIMITED."[24]

Deep within the highland rainforests, the Maya have the sweetest little bees, not much bigger than the very tip of your smallest finger. They do not even have stingers. Beautiful winged creatures, they are in harmony with the orchids, cultivating the nectar and producing honey for the community. The Maya know that because the bees are so very delicate and the hives so small, they can only harvest one tablespoon of honey per year from a hive. That honey becomes very precious medicine.

The Maya tell us we are ending the time of the People of Maize and becoming the people of honey. People of Maize need to take from the earth in order to live. They need to dig in their heels and plant something, forcing it to grow. They worry if the rain will come, if insects will infect the crops, if the harvest will yield enough. From this place of fear and lack, the People of Maize end up stealing, begging or blaming.

When the Maya say we are becoming the People of Honey, the larger context is that we are returning to a state of exquisite balance and harmony for all of humanity. The time of honey is the golden age that has been spoken about by so many. It is a level of harmony we have not yet enjoyed because of the ego imbalance present in the way of the maize people.

Honey is a gift offered through the beauty of flowers. It is an essence, an offering of love. When we allow ourselves to embrace our authentic selves, to welcome each other as the people of honey, we let go of the energy of fear, lack and blame. Together, we see the beauty, we are nourished by the nectar and we enter a time of acceptance and bounty.

Honey is essence; aligning with one's essential nature is the act that offers this nectar. Honey is gathered from a flower, and it comes at the appropriate time for a particular plant. We are like the plants, each having its own gestation time before the harvest. As you read this book, smile. It is your time to flower, to offer breath and nectar to the world.

Your Self-Ascension is in service to the soul and to humanity as the sweetest nectar. It is a welcoming of the time of honey. You will not ascend until you are ready to fully embrace and remember who you are while you still have a beautiful body.

As we move toward the abundant nature of living as the people of honey, the remnants of our history as the people of maize is before us. It is the resolution of this closure that offers the tipping point of our collective future and our yearning for stability.

The word *authenticity* carries with it many connotations. Within the core essence of your soul connection is the ability to discover the deeper truth beyond your mind of density. This truth offers conscious authenticity, or alignment with the soul. One practical gateway to the soul is simply to follow your joy.

Choosing actions that align with the truth of your joy, outside of the emotional mandates, is an action of a person of honey. It comes from the effervescence discovered when you release all need to control, and simply claim yourself at the core of where your joy lies. From this space your actions align with this choice and a natural flow comes forward. The celebration of completion can be understood while the revelation of the future unfolds.

☀ ☀ ☀

A special message from the Benevolent Ones:

"Infinite blessings of love and joy are showered to you on this day of momentous recognition.

Every day is a day of momentous recognition, and with each conscious connection to this gift, the shower of love and joy that you choose to receive expands infinitely.

Allowing yourself to RECEIVE the shower of love and joy that is in all-ways available is a step toward the continuous gift of recognition that ALL EXPERIENCES of MIRACLES are in all-ways possible.

Understand beloved ones: The true miracle is the calling forth of your focus without distraction from the illusion.

As a being of infinite expression and expansion, the only force that can deny your miraculous power of manifestation is your lack of focus upon this gift. Stray emotions, discordant energies, judgments, are just a few of the available venues to distract you.

FOCUS upon your recognition. FOCUS upon your miracle intent. FOCUS upon your expression as a being of infinite love in form.

And as you FOCUS, your MIRACLES unfold as does the collective miracle of planetary shift at a moment of great distraction.

Indeed, today is a day of momentous recognition! You must focus to claim the harmony of your life! This begins with the release of doubt that you are here as a Divine being having an experience of life!"

❄ ❄ ❄

There is a great gift in allowing yourself to focus. Through the Clarity Mantra found in Chapter One you are able to fully expand into the gift of self-trust. Let us now add the focus attribute to this powerful mantra and dive with love into the time of the people of honey.

The FOCUS Formula

Follow your guidance; discern the voice of guidance, not mind chatter.

Open your heart; listen inwardly, relax the mind.

Claim your truth; trust in action.

Understand *all* experience in the bigger picture. Accept the perfection.

Simplify your life. Prioritize! Allow for unlimited divine spaciousness.

With each moment you are navigating the culmination of the People of Maize, and it can look like conflict and chaos, love and hate, joy and fear. With all the apparent polarities, the world may seem unstable. Yet, even with the chaotic events in our economy and political scene, even with uncertain financial security, the extraordinary news is that there is emerging an increased human capacity to cultivate true peace. This is the gift of these times. First take a moment and try this: take a deep breath right now and let it out with a loud audible sigh. Bring your hand to your heart and take another even deeper breath; relax further. The gift of these breaths brings you into the peaceful present moment. Even if your mind was filled with racing thoughts, taking two or three conscious breaths will stabilize your emotions and open the doorway to inner peace.

So what about our world? When we gaze upon terror attacks and experience weak economic structures, the inner results can be very unsettling. News reports are filled with fear. Yet these very situations are a call to sanity, a call to awaken to a richer and deeper truth. The

THE BEGINNING OF THE PEOPLE OF HONEY

chaos in our world is actually an evolutionary sign when we focus with clarity!

Ready or not, the world is reawakening from an ancient dream. Consciousness is expanding beyond traditional beliefs and structures. Our notions of power, integrity and co-creation are all evolving. Our world is indeed in transition. Polarity and unrest are increasing and time is speeding up. Chaos is the norm, for this transition is shaking the energetic foundation of all beings.

As our bodies try to integrate higher frequency energy, many people are reporting vision changes, interrupted sleep patterns and impatience with in-authenticity. We are experiencing a "Global wake-up call" and that call is to a higher form of integrity and clarity. We are at the time of great choice, the time to fully embrace our authentic soul energy without any doubt.

To benefit from the chaos, we must release our attachments to worldly expectations, traditional beliefs and many mental patterns. This initially feels destabilizing until you open more fully to the energy of your core essence—your soul. That opening is most easily cultivated by bringing your hand to your heart and breathing deeply. This simple practice will connect your consciousness to your Soul. You can indeed find your center in the face of turmoil if you choose to.

HOW CAN WE PROPERLY PREPARE FOR WHAT WE CANNOT EVEN IMAGINE?

Instead of focusing on the chaos of these times, instead of feeding the mind on uncertainty, let us use the chaos to remind us to claim our mastery. The outer world will not ever offer stability, but it can remind you to direct your seeking inward. Then your soul can better guide you. Each being has all the wisdom they require, if they will listen inwardly through their own heart centers.

This listening cultivates self-trust and empowers authenticity. This inner path is compatible with all spiritual beliefs and offers true blessings in abundance. As we listen inwardly our guidance becomes ever more clear. As the mind lets the soul lead the way, new revelations and understandings come forward effortlessly.

Everyone is feeling the energetic shift that is happening globally. The chaos and fear around is positioned to rapidly escalate. Yet within this intensity many are aligning with their core essence for the first time; a great celebration!

Your core essence offers you the ability to feel things you have never felt before. You will touch things you have not ever touched before. How you break free and navigate these core feelings will be influenced by your habitual reactionary system. To navigate these energies, you must release the habit of pain-based beliefs.

The energy of these times will provoke inner healing for those who are ready to awaken. The opportunity is before us all to claim our authentic empowerment. The chaos of transformation is affecting all beings on this planet and many will notice shifts in their pets or other animals as well.

You cannot navigate for others. There is nothing you can do to shift them. They each must find their own way, and as you navigate authentically, your presence will inspire authenticity in them. It is that simple. Navigating the chaos is not difficult; it simply requires presence through your clarity and consistent focus.

How and where is your future to go? Are you open to trusting your inner wisdom?

Try this: bring your hand to your heart, breathe deeply and relax. Then pick up a pen and write across the top of the page, "What do I need to know for the coming years?" Relax your mind and free-associate messages from your inner wisdom. Just let the writing flow. Later, as you read what was written, a deeper understanding will come forward.

You can also call forth your core essence each morning by declaring a clear and focused "thank you" upon arising. From this energy of gratitude, you will dissolve chaos into clarity. It is a wondrous time to be alive. Enjoy the transformation!

Now is the time to fully harness the power of the mantra of Self-Ascension with each breath, and it is as simple as:

I AM HERE
I AM READY
I AM OPEN
GUIDE ME.

Your Miracle Moment

This message is from the Ascended Masters of Lake Atitlán:

Circles of Divine energy are swirling around your world now. These circles are seen by some as spirals and by others as orbs, yet they are one energy that is calling forth the time of the resurrection of the lost worlds that are regenerating on and through your world with each breath a conscious being takes.

We wish for you not to engage the word lost with any translation other than that which recognizes cycles are the gift of birth and transformation. When a new cycle births often the energies that were important during that time become "lost" in the time that has arisen.

Each cycle carries with it the many gifts that bring forth culmination so that the next cycle may begin. You are at the moment and the hour of the Divine culmination and the birth of transmutation in its full form of Conscious reunion.

THIS IS A MIRACLE and one that has been patiently waiting and lovingly nurtured for many years by those few of your world who were connected to its stream of conscious energy. ALL who choose are now ready to re-enter this stream, AND not all will choose to do so. Yet another miracle of the world of choice!

Shortly your perception of time will end one year and begin another... the circles are swirling and the energies are building. Take note of where you are called to be, smile at the closure upon your world and the birth that is already in process.

With great love we share this with you so that your hearts may open ever wider to the expanded energies that have been waiting for you to remember and to reclaim as the effortless process of navigating through all perception. Breathe and know that all is well and that the water of all life surrounds you with love!

Chapter Seven

MEETING THE
OFF-WORLDERS

"YOU are the expansion of Light."[25]

Sit back, relax for a moment and join us on a journey. Everything you are about to read is 100 percent true (as is everything else in this book). Had we not personally witnessed and participated in these extraordinary events, we ourselves might have been skeptical that they could all occur. And yet, when the shaman's journey appears, none can deny it.

Living within the dream of this world experience and settled into our everyday routines, one can easily forget that there are simultaneous worlds. There are numerous "unidentified" experiences unfolding around us at any given moment. When we do reflect upon

off-worlders, we are usually reflecting upon those whom we perceive to originate from other planets, solar systems or universes. Yet
within our everyday experience, we are *all* directly interacting with
off-worlders in one way or another.

For us, it began in Machu Pichu, Peru, in September 2005. Having been called to this mystical journey we had no idea it was setting
the stage for a secret, yet very open meeting with the off-worlders.

Kira Raa shortly after an Archangelic connection at Machu Pichu.

Local children offering gifts and smiles gather around Kira Raa
shortly after divine connections.

Standing near the top of the ancient site in Peru, as Kira gazed out between two mountain ranges, she was transported to the headwaters of the Ganges in India…across the world! To witness her experience as she watched the dimensions fold and space collide with what we perceive as time was simultaneously fascinating and a bit frightening.

Her body swayed dangerously back and forth, eyes wide open, and she mumbled that there was an energetic connection between the Himalayas and the Andes. Then as if nothing had happened, she turned, gazed lovingly at Sri Ram Kaa and said, "One day we will go to India to continue this journey."

That *one day* became December 17, 2008, well after we had already discovered the highlands of Guatemala and the elders of the Mayan tribes. Three years later, at the headwaters of the Ganges, a promise was kept from that first magical moment in Machu Pichu and later reconfirmed through the Ascended Master St. Germaine.[26]

Arriving at the headwaters of the Ganges, the air was clear, the river stunning, and the Himalayas captivating. The world once again became a distant journey as the dimensions folded, time stood still, and a powerful portal appeared before Sri and Kira revealing what looked like an ancient one. He was dressed fully in white, and had a golden glow that fully enveloped him. He was rising about 10 feet above the Ganges, and his presence was as real as any person who would ever stand before you. He said only one thing: "Return to Guatemala and complete this journey."

And then he seemed to simply vanish as the sun once again illuminated the Ganges. The world suddenly had sound, wind and other people.

This beautiful contact felt more real than any earthly experience. We felt drawn to come to India, yet this one's message was for us to return to Guatemala. We knew it was time to further understand how these very tangible messages would integrate for us. Childlike excitement filled us as we realized that we were drawing closer to the moment to sit in full consciousness with the off-worlders.

A group filled with divine energy attracts large crowds
shortly after divine connections.

Our time in India was extraordinary on so many levels, yet a great sadness would consistently overwhelm us. Perhaps it was the terrorist attack at Mumbai that now had all the sacred temples at a level of vigilance that made airport security seem mild. None of the famous sacred sites were available to simply sit and be with. You were herded through and not allowed to linger. If you decided to pause and just appreciate the energy, as Kira did when she arrived at Krishna's birthplace in Vrindavan, you were politely but sternly reminded to keep moving.

It seemed to signify a greater movement in the energy or the spiritual heart center of the planet. Everywhere we went in India, we easily witnessed ceremonies and rituals. Yet, within each one there seemed to be the energy of obligation rather than the authentic love and devotion of the experience.

Certainly that love and devotion does exist, and India is a rich and stunning experience that is not to be missed. However to be there with Kira Raa, and share with her in the revisiting of places she has lived before, walking streets she had not been to in this lifetime, yet knowing every alley, every brick, was somewhat intimidating. Like a ghost haunting a building we touched ancient times through an intangible sense of timelessness.

We were now in Varanasi, the holiest place on the planet for Hindus, where many Hindus go to transition. We were walking the streets just after sunrise, and without warning Kira was barely able to walk the streets.

She was experiencing many disincarnate beings, so many that she started waving her hands to try and get them to clear a path. In that moment, the third dimension and the astral-bound off-worlders melded as one. So many lost souls had congregated here. When we finally did arrive at the Ganges, she just dropped and cried. The combination of the heavily polluted water and the congestion of the disincarnates was overwhelming.

Then "he" appeared to her again, beautiful, illuminated and comforting, once again floating over the water of the Ganges. It simply reminded Kira, "Return to Guatemala and do not despair. All is in perfect order, and you will find the answers there."

The morning shores of Varnasi already busy with the holy work of the day.

Tears of joy and relief streamed down our faces. Without this visitation we do not know how we would have continued on the journey of Varanasi, and we were many blocks away from our van and many hours from leaving. Through loving clarity, this off-world visitor offered us a sense of reassurance, and we were ready to honor this gift. We had an inner sense that India had offered all she could give, and we relaxed further into trust.

Returning to the U.S. from India, we found it challenging to settle back into any form of a "normal" routine. Guatemala was calling us, and just one month after returning, we boarded a plane for the Land of Eternal Spring. We had not yet discussed our visitations openly with each other, and yet we both felt a heightened sense of peace and reconnection as the plane drew closer to our destination.

Our residence at Lake Atitlán was not yet ready for occupancy, so we rented a hotel room at a lovely small hotel just a few miles from our small Mayan village. We arrived late in the afternoon, and were tired on many levels. Knowing that "something" was ahead the next day, we chose a light, early dinner and went to bed with the setting of the sun.

As we rose the next morning, the sun was unusually brilliant and the lake was like a mirror. Often there are winds that can create amazing waves on the lake or shimmering ripples, yet today, she was as tranquil as we had ever experienced her. The luminescence of the sun was especially brilliant on the one smaller volcano on the lake known as Cerro de Oro, the hill of gold. History tells us that when the early Spaniards arrived, many Maya were killed for refusing to reveal where the gold was on this beautiful little mountain. In truth, the mountain *is* the gold. When the sun illuminates it, one can easily see the beauty that reveals itself.

From our hotel room balcony, we had a first-rate view of this mountain of gold, illuminated now with such extraordinary hues that we simply sat, mesmerized, until the phone rang. We sat captivated by the beauty for over an hour before our boat taxi arrived to take us to TOSA La Laguna. It was obvious we were already being prepared for something, and our joy increased with each passing minute.

From the hotel dock we boarded our boat still enjoying the view of that Cerro de Orro across the lake. Holding our gaze steady at the small mountain, we inhaled the breeze of the boat as it cut through the glasslike surface of the water. Without warning, we began to feel friction in our energy, as if we were pushing through a piece of plastic wrap.

The beauty of the Mountain of Gold, one of the smallest volcanoes at Lake Atitlán.

And then, just when the plastic wrap felt as if it would compress our breath, there was a "pop," as if we had just burst through a veil, and we noticed we were now past the little mountain and everything, literally everything, was shimmering! It was like taking a breath for the very first time. Huge smiles lit up our faces as we gazed at each other with knowing looks. Yes! The lake was preparing to reveal something to us, and the journey from Machu Pichu to India and back was about to culminate before us.

A friend of ours, who owned a large home still under construction just before TOSA La Laguna, had asked us to stop by on our way over. We quietly brought the boat to the front of the house.

"Sri, I'm not sure why, but we need to go up to that window, right there," Kira said, pointing to a second-story window frame that was waiting to have its large central window fitted in.

"Sure, my love, let's go," affirmed Sri.

We climbed the stairs of the truly magnificent unfinished home and arrived in what we assumed would become some form of master bedroom. The room itself was stark and quite large, and the central fireplace was even larger. Due to the extensive size of the house, it had taken several minutes to reach our destination once we had disembarked from the boat. Gazing out the window, we had not noticed that a gentle mist had appeared from what felt like nowhere and settled around the house and the lake.

As Kira positioned herself on the open window ledge, Sri kept a close distance, as a fall from this height could easily be fatal. Quickly, Kira began communicating with the energies and the off-worlders that were there, and just a few moments later, with tears in her eyes, she turned to Sri and shared:

"There is a beautiful goddess of this lake, and she is crying. She is right there"—Kira was pointing out to a specific spot on the lake— "and she is saying that she has revealed herself to others before, and that they have not responded."

The energy of loving connection was tangible as Kira continued, "She is also sharing that the lake is dying and that her world will die with it unless the Legions of Light re-emerge and are supported

Kira Raa moments after her communion with the Goddess of the Lake.

by those who are in body now and can communicate with her. She asked me if we were coming to offer this support, and I said yes. Sri, we must do this, there is more here than just this. I feel as if this is the just the first piece of a very large puzzle."

Sri immediately responded, "So, lets get over to TOSA La Laguna and be present for the revelation. It feels like we have what we needed from this spot and that this was the reason we needed to stop by here." Kira smiled and held out her hand as Sri helped her from the window.

Quietly, and with great reverence, we once again boarded our boat. We could barely contain our excitement to once again be on the gentle land that would anchor the gift of Self-Ascension at this very special spot on our planet.

The moment we entered the lagoon, we knew we were heading straight to the Merkabah deck. Words were not needed as we sent our boat driver away and climbed the few steps to the deck. The air was warm and filled with the rising mist, yet there was a vivid clarity of light.

Sri sat quietly. Kira was already deep in connection when they both experienced the same energy that we had found at the Ganges.

A large ball of light came forward from directly in front of the deck, and the majestic illuminated being appeared again.

"Welcome. It has been a long time as it has been no time. Before you is the Crystalline City of the Ascended Masters, an abode of light that has intentionally hidden from your world until this moment of revelation. We ask that you not share our existence until one year from now, thereby offering to yourself and to us the stabilization of the lifting of the city, and the reunification of the energies of your planet as she adjusts to her new spine. Behold before you the golden doors that hold the energy of the city."

Kira began weeping as the beauty and the profound power of the energy of the city beamed upon us. The doors gently began to open. At first the light was so bright that eyes of this world were unable to gaze at it. We both adjusted our vision and were offered a glimpse of the beauty of the city and the wisdom that it was holding.

Our visitor continued: "Your world has come to a moment of great choice once again, and our silence is no longer warranted. There are many abodes of Ascended Masters that will soon be revealed that have also been cloaked for the ages. The abodes of past now operate as holograms for those who are just awakening. Many will still gather at those abodes and claim to see us, and indeed they are, only through the gift of holographic projection. At the time of the millennium we came together to arrive at our cities of light that would carry the energy of the future of your world with them. This is the capitol of those cities, the place where we all gather and where we rejuvenate. There will be many revelations that will come forward from this city, and from here the great energy of the new spine of Gaia will be anchored as we resurrect the heartbeat of all humanity. Many of us are here that you already know by name, and many of us have not been revealed to your world until now. This does not matter. What matters is that the moment has arrived, and that you have honored the call. There is much ahead, and for now it is best to simply acclimate to the energy here, and allow the action of patience to restore you and your world."

Had we heard correctly? Had we just experienced and seen a new abode of the ascended masters? The overwhelming energy of the moment was almost too much to bear. We sat, we cried, we smiled and we realized that once again our journey was just beginning.

When one touches the truth of the off-worlders in all of their forms and can lovingly accept that we live in a multi-dimensional reality, there is a sense of authentic sanity that emerges.

Yet there is a presence and a gift to ascended sanity, and it is a key piece to experiencing your full freedom and sharing your highest service without any reservation. The heart knows what the mind can not yet comprehend. Archangel Zadkiel explained to us one day that: *"Those who choose density they will not ever see you as sane. And those who choose awakening, will discover an ever expanding experience through their ascended sanity beyond density."*

Your Miracle Moment

This message is from the Benevolent Ones and the Brethren of Light:

With great presence and love we beseech thee to see beyond the limited self. Open your hearts to the expansiveness of Divine presence expressed through all expressions in form and without form.

The limited view of the "self" alone has come to the moment where it will bring forth great challenges as it struggles to survive and protect itself in a world that has already entered into a new cycle.

Within your inidivid-u-will life expressions you will begin to find the challenges ever more expressive if your mind continues on a singular journey of me-ness. This expression, of course, serves to bring you to a greater truth and the greater expression.

*Release any judgment of your journey and the path
will open!*

*To fully move into the recognition that each being of love,
when expressing through their wholeness, supports ALL
BEINGS OF LOVE, then the challenges quickly dissipate and
the awakened revelations come forward with abundance.*

Chapter Eight

LiViNG WitH
ASCENDED SANitY

"WHEN i DESPAiR, i REMEMBER THAT ALL THROUGH
HiSTORY THE WAY OF TRUTH AND LOVE HAS ALWAYS
WON. THERE HAVE BEEN TYRANTS AND MURDERERS,
AND FOR A TiME THEY SEEM iNViNCiBLE, BUT iN THE
END, THEY ALWAYS FALL—THiNK OF iT, ALWAYS."[27]

In March, 2009, we were hosting 30 eager, demanding spiritual seek-
ers who traveled to Guatemala to understand the greater energies of
the Mayan calendar, 2012 and the "heart" of the Americas. This trip
from the very beginning was different, mystical, magical and revelatory. We had offered our guests advance warning that the purity of

the energy here would stimulate movement in everyone. We had no idea how strong those reactions would be.

While busily shuttling our tour group through sights in the colonial capital city of Antigua, we received a phone call from our good friend and Mayan priestess Amanda, saying, "He knows you are here, and he wants to meet with you."

"Who?" we asked.

"Don Maya, the elders' elder of the Maya. He is now 84 and is ready to meet with you and your group in Tikal for a very special ceremony," Amanda shared in a serious tone. We were surprised and delighted that this elder was awaiting further connection with us.

It would be another week before we arrived in Tikal, and we knew then that the unfolding energies of the off-worlders had already come forward once again. There was an air of sacred preparation and preparatory sacrifice amongst everyone in the group.

The week unfolded with strange events. There was the group of nine who were guided to transverse a mountain cliff on behalf of all. They were the first group of international visitors ever to sit in the sacred cave of the wind and perform ceremony. Returning to the larger group that evening they were exhausted, some with minor injuries, yet their spirits soared with the magic of the experience.

Then there was the traveler who decided to simply leave the group. As he was missing for days without any communication, we had missing person posters all over the lakeshore and had notified the U.S. Embassy. On our last day, he returned to the group with his body covered in black writing, a jar of black dirt in his hands.

The high priests of the village informed us that he had fallen prey to dark, ancient Mayan energy from one of the villages that eagerly awaits stray tourists. The curse that had been placed on him was designed to steal his soul and then infiltrate the group with negative energy. In the past, this type of experience had literally led to murder. Black magic can have tangible and serious consequences if your energy field is open to its influence.

Upon his return, filled with a fascinating combination of rage and self-importance, he grabbed his girlfriend and left again. Twenty-four hours later, when they tried to return, four members of the group stood strong as guardians in their clarity to refuse interference energies and asked them both to leave the group.

Later that same day, a woman who had been afraid to feel her emotions or let go of her business persona received the break she had been reaching out for. While returning from an outing across the lake, the boat that held us was being tossed across the very high waves like a small cork.

Arriving at the dock, the boat would dance with the waves, lifting high above the dock, and, a moment later, diving deep below it. Self-preoccupied, she decided to exit the boat before it was properly tied.

"Wait for the helper!" we all cried out as she began to jump from the boat.

We all watched in horror as her foot caught between the dock and the lurching boat and literally twisted her ankle into a new position 90 degrees from normal. Everyone was silent as she looked at us in denial and obvious shock.

A wave of healer energy and love quickly surrounded her as we attempted to make her comfortable on the dock. Sri immediately placed healing energy around the broken bones while a makeshift gurney was constructed to take her to a doctor.

She left on another boat, never to return to the group. Her break had arrived. Her remaining days were spent in a hospital in Guatemala City, where she underwent orthopedic surgery and retreated back to the United States. These events were a foreshadowing, a trial. Guatemala was indeed stimulating a healing for the entire group, and now it was time to leave for Tikal.

The week between the notification of meeting Don Maya and arriving in Tikal had been filled with many merged energies of this world and another. Those who were not ready had been cleansed from the group. Those who were ready had the experience of living fully and opening to the off-worlder energy firsthand, whether they believed it was possible or not. There was a new sense of peace and harmony within the group. We were all prepared, and little did we know this journey had just begun.

After spending over a week with 30 tourists in the highlands of Guatemala, many of whom had never been outside the U.S., we were already feeling the exhaustion of attending to the needs of so many. Attending to the vast needs of the group would have been enough, however with the "strange" events we had all just live through, and the energetic focus we were all offering, the group arrived at the charter hangar at the airport in Guatemala City ready to relax.

Amanda, our good friend and Mayan priestess, had arranged for a private charter flight to bring our group to Tikal. She and Don Maya were already aware of the many strange and fascinating experiences the group had gone through during the week since we had last communicated. They were also aware that not everyone who had originally intended to come with us to Tikal would be arriving there.

Walking out to the runway, the ancient charter planes—probably discards from the U.S. commercial fleet—did not inspire confidence. Yet we knew without a doubt that we would be safe. Once inside the plane, we had to smile as we had never seen so much duct tape on a plane. Good thing it works so well.

Flying at low altitude in the bumpy clouds with little ventilation on the plane was yet another initiation for those on the journey to Tikal. With motion sickness bags in hand, many silent prayers for calmer skies were uttered. The sight of the small runway in Flores drew applause and a sigh of relief from us all.

Stepping from the plane onto the runway, we discovered it was not just hot in Flores, it was scorching hot! It felt as if a giant blow dryer had been directed toward us. Walking into the one-room terminal without air conditioning was a new experience of patience and tolerance for very tired travelers. In the midst of such personal discomfort, one finds the surrender to the greater experience, and one climbs into their ascended sanity.

There was an air of unspoken excitement and understanding that this excursion was beyond anything physical. What would have turned back even the most experienced traveler was becoming a tempting mystery to unfold. Driving from Flores to the archaeological zone of Tikal was silent, reflective, hot and emotional. We had already put in a full eight-hour day of travel that started with a boat,

An orb-filled sunrise at Tikal.

then a van, then the plane, then another van. Rest and a comfortable bed were on everyone's mind and with good reason.

Arriving at the jungle lodge, everyone began to disburse to their respective rooms. As we entered our simple room we were instantly reminded that we were in the middle of the rainforest. Gazing around, our first greeting was from the scorpion climbing our curtains. "He" turned out to be just the first of our bedroom creatures, which also included centipedes, a myriad of flying insects, tarantulas and other assorted large spiders.

Finally arranging the mosquito netting around the bed and triple checking the sheets for stowaways, we felt a long overdue late afternoon nap converge upon us. Relaxing into the recognition that there were no longer any insect friends in or near our bed, the gift of sleep began to set in.

At that moment, loud knocking startled us. It was forceful and overbearing, the type of knocking that makes your heart pound and your breath stop. Half-dressed, we staggered to the door and opened it to find Amanda standing there, demanding, "Come. Now. We must go now!"

Sri was so exhausted he could barely move, so Kira mustered the strength to leave with Amanda in her very worn jungle jeep. The strangely out-of-place music of Jethro Tull's *Aqualung* was blasting from the vehicle as Amanda drove off in a frenzy with Kira trapped and jostled inside.

"Where are we going?" Kira asked, not sure if she would be heard over the music.

"We must manifest a miracle. This is why you must be with me. Don Maya says the ceremony must be today and it must be now! But Tikal closes at five p.m., and we don't have a permit to enter the park after hours. And there are a lot of people in your group. We're going to meet with the park officials right now and make this happen." She spoke quickly, and the music kept getting louder with each thump over the pitted dirt road.

"Okay, if this is to be, then let us get it done," responded Kira, feeling half like a prisoner and half an adventurer, holding on for dear life as every turn threw her from her seat.

The Tikal guard, a small Maya, looked up lazily as we walked in. He listened as Amanda threw down a piece of paper and in very quick Spanish told him our needs and the importance of the ceremony. Rolling his eyes, and totally disinterested, he feigned an argument and picked up his radio to call someone else.

Knowing the importance of the needed permit, Kira mustered the last of her energy, looked at him, smiled and simply gazed at his eyes. He put down his radio, and with the stroke of a pen, granted the permit.

Walking out the door, Amanda shared with Kira, "You see, you are in Tikal. The ancestors know you are here and want to see you. That's why the permit was given."

Amanda continued talking urgently as she drove like a fireman. "We must go now! You go get Sri Ram Kaa and I will get Don Maya and the ceremony supplies. I'll pick you both up in five minutes."

Driving back into the entrance of the jungle lodge, Kira had no choice but to shout out the windows to members of the group, "We are going for the ceremony now. Find everyone and meet us in five minutes."

Was this really happening?

Five minutes later we were back in the car with the Maya elder of elders, Don Maya, and on our way to the site he had specifically chosen for the ceremony. The group had walking directions, and it would take them about 30 minutes to walk the trail through Tikal and meet up with us. We were stunned that Amanda had the permission and determination to simply drive where "no one drives" deep into the park.

Sunset was soon upon us. As we arrived at the sacred, ancient altar site in front of a pyramid far away from the main Tikal tourist sites, we were struck by the small sign explaining that the altar had been in continuous use from 532 AD until 2006 AD, when all ceremony was prohibited.

Don Maya gazed at this chosen site as we were offloading many boxes of offerings and ceremonial supplies. He quietly, slowly, lit up a hand-rolled cigar and began puffing it, and intermittently he would take it from his mouth and gaze upon it. After doing this a few times, he went up to the small sign that claimed ceremony could not be performed here, and with one effortless pull, yanked it from the ground and threw it to the side. It was obvious the cigar claimed that site for the evening's ceremony.

Don Maya was now in full swing, preparing for the ceremony. It was hard to believe he was 84 years old. The deftness, certainty, mental acuity and precision with which he unfolded the ceremony was beyond impressive. As he would hand us copal to prepare, or handmade candles to unwind from their long strings, he would constantly keep lighting cigars, reading the smoke and the way the tobacco burned. Then he would return his attention to us making sure we were preparing the sacred ceremony properly.

As our group arrived, Don Maya asked us to stop them from entering the sacred site until he read his cigar. A few puffs later he called us over with the motion of an old wrinkled finger and smiled broadly and toothlessly as he pointed to the cigar.

"This," he said, "is a sign they can enter. Do you see this?"

Gazing at the side of the cigar, we saw a perfect round circle that had burned through the side of the cigar.

"Yes, the circle," we responded.

He shook his finger in the air, smiled, and then pointed up and said, "An important night. An important ceremony."

Despite their obvious fatigue, our group entered the sacred circle with reverence, joy and the energy of anticipation. We all stood around the very large circular ceremonial altar that was filled to the brim with offerings. Don Maya entered into the center of the group, got down on his knees and kissed the ground. Everyone did the same, there was no need to explain what was happening or to follow any rules. The gift of synergy was in divine flow, and the fire began.

There is a phenomenon that happens with authentic ceremony. Time seems to stand still as you find yourself mesmerized by the actions of the fire and the hypnotic chanting of ancient language by the high priests and elders. This night was no exception. The difference was that we were standing in the middle of Tikal, at an ancient altar, and the sounds of the jungle became more pronounced as the evening became darker and darker. This was indeed a privilege.

It is one thing to hear the sounds of the jungle in a movie or zoo. It is quite another to be in the middle of the jungle, without any form of protection except spirit, and experience these sounds. The backdrop of the sounds of the monkeys, birds and insects would have been deafening if the fire had not been so large and so vocal.

We were all in a flow of energy communion, mystery and sensation. Time stood still. The mind stopped. Smoke, flames and a sense of reverence remained. Without full awareness of how it happened, we were now several hours into the ceremony, and overhead the stars were forming amazing patterns—or were they stars? Do stars move like that? Do stars shift with the rise of the smoke and the ignition of the fire?

About five of us decided to look up, following the plumes of aromatic smoke into the night sky. The light show we experienced will never be forgotten. The off-worlders were speaking in yet another language, and we were delighted to be the witnesses of this display.

Once again we were being gifted with an experience that challenges all the rules of sanity according to our everyday world view. A shamanic ceremony evokes ancient knowing from deep within. The guardians of this site opened the doorways, and their cosmic brethren gathered. All sense of time had faded into a captivating timelessness of now. The group members were all touched and each had a personal and private experience. The fire is a unifying energy. It offers a resurrection of spirit not found within air-conditioned walls.

Don Maya walked over to Kira at this point and reached up to place his hand on her shoulder, quietly saying, "Pay attention. They are here with a great message."

"I know," Kira whispered.

He continued, "This ceremony has been received by the ancestors. Soon your time of greater communion with them will arrive and this group tonight was here only as a witness." And with that, Don Maya began stirring what was left of the fire.

Our hearts were thrown open, and tears were flowing down Sri's, Kira's and Amanda's faces. With cheeks streaked with tears, we felt the honor of this moment. We all felt a deeper sense of peace and trust in our own beingness and our interconnectivity. There was no doubt at all, the off-worlders had spoken, the ascended masters were present and the heart of the Americas was calling out to be heard.

❀ ❀ ❀

To step into your Ascended Sanity is to walk through *all* of the paradigms of density without looking back. It is not an easy journey, and very few will support you along they way. How can they? For they honestly have no idea what you are experiencing. How can you describe Self-Revelation, Creative Action and Abundant Expansion?

How can you explain your great trust in the universe? The truth is you cannot. You can only live it.

It is through your consistent commitment to living in Ascended Sanity that eventually those who have been worried about you along the way will relax into the recognition that you have shifted. You are not just in some phase! You are truly living in a state of awakened presence that is supporting you. The gift of your consistent and committed actions is that regardless of their understanding, those in density will finally accept you for who you are. And with that, your presence may free others who choose to do the same! They may not understand you, however a sense of respect for your Ascended Sanity will emerge.

Until that time, there is truly one wonderful phrase to guide your journey:

"Forgive them, they know not what they do."

—*Luke 23:34, The Bible*

This is an important discernment, for how can you hold anyone accountable when they are fully asleep to the impact of their actions? This does not excuse them from actions of atrocity; it does, however, assist you to stay committed to your growth.

As we embrace Ascended Sanity, we begin to understand how we create and re-create drama in our lives. We find the energy to break free from limiting beliefs. This is a great gift, as we are awake enough to look lovingly at ourselves without judging ourselves. We then stop judging the outer world. The level of consciousness of those who wage war prevents them from fully apprehending their actions.

Claiming our own trust, we are able to see more clearly. We come to discover our true needs on an emotional, physical and spiritual basis. We are free of the imposed limitations that seek to tell us what to believe and how to act. When we act from the highest connection of spirit, we understand our personal triggers and how to take action to fully embrace our life with passionate action.

This is, of course, the ultimate secret—harnessing this energy of Ascended Sanity to create abundant manifest flow for our lives. We do this through expansionary Self-Ascension practices[28] and techniques.

As with any spiritual practice, the gift of the practice will bring us to the opening of our heart.

In the first chapter of this book we introduced you to the clarity mantra. This is just one practice that can assist you along your journey. As you grow on your journey, you can expand this practice with just three simple steps, and you must begin with asking yourself the question: *What do I really want?*

This powerful question can stimulate fear, anxiety and downright panic. The most common response to this question is, "I want abundance" in some form. True abundance is elusive for many. Even those with abundant financial resources may experience lack and fear. There is a preoccupation with not trusting ourselves; leading to the bigger question: *Why are we often fearful and unclear?*

True abundance offers essential harmony experienced as peace with oneself and one's world, the foundation for manifestation. One is unable to manifest from the energy of fear and lack, which are density energies. Regardless of how many self-help coaches suggest otherwise, lack of material wealth is a spiritual challenge requiring a healing solution.

Here are three simple steps that will free your doubt as you claim radiant abundance.

Step One: All wounds are healed through love. Accept that doubt energy can be healed. This reclaims your manifesting power. Imagine what your life would be like if had no doubts...about anything. Self-love offers self-acceptance. Accept your life as a divine gift. Bring your hand to your heart and declare: "In this moment I trust myself!" Breathe in the energy of self-trust and let it flow into your cells.

Step Two: Bring both your hands to your heart and ask: "Beloved Spirit, show me where I am holding the wound of self-judgment." State this command out loud with trust and authority. Allow one hand to float over your body and find a resting place that calls to you. This creates a healing circuit, a link from your heart. Breathe deeply and allow love and trust to flow between your hands. Breathe with gratitude and accept the flow of love.

Step Three: Hand to heart, declare: "I am the Healing Light of the Divine, and I now release and transmute all discord and limitation."

Take your time with this exercise and allow it to transform years of negative patterning. Gift yourself by repeating Steps One to Three daily for three weeks, and you will see marvelous results in your life. As you acquire the habit of trusting yourself and releasing doubt, finding the gifts in your life become ever more joyful as you step further and further into your Ascended Sanity.

Stepping fully into Ascended Sanity, you recognize that you have the ability to command spirit. Instead of coming from a sense of lack, you instead command the light from a place of empowered trust. As you harness this ability you can effortlessly transmute all discord, energize your Attractor Field with wholeness and delight as you empower the experience of true abundance.

An important moment in your growth will arise as you claim your clarity and step further into Ascended Sanity. In that moment, either your ego or the ego of others will project upon you a sense of specialness. Believing that you are special is a delusion that can carry you back into the flow of density consciousness. This is an important discernment that must be addressed. Many who have empowered their mystical gifts or touched the ascended realms drift back into density consciousness, thereby adding to the global chaos despite their claims of being special.

The ego then steps forward to claim the sense of specialness and willingly allows itself to be influenced by energies that feed its need. The question will arise: How do I know if I am being interfered with?

We asked this same question of Archangel Zadkiel, and here was the inspired response:

SRI RAM KAA: How can one know when they are receiving information that is based in density consciousness and interfering with their clarity?

ARCHANGEL ZADKIEL: *It is only doubt can disconnect one from their being-ness. When one allows the energy of doubt to permeate their consciousness, they have allowed the opening of a portal that will be attractive to chaotic interference, and Astral energies will find the portal to enter.*

Once this interference energy has anchored itself, often you are unable to discern that it is present.

To move through this energy takes great self-determination and transparency. Remember, the goal of this energy is to Interfere, and it was welcomed in! Only through allowing your heart to fully anchor its presence and through releasing the egoic filter that will want to hold firmly to the energy of interference, will you release it. The egoic filter most times enjoys the interference since often this energy will cater to the ego to stay present.

You are able to walk through this interference energy if you remain in the wholeness of Self-Ascension and release self-judgment. You are able to fully anchor on the other side. It is simply important for you to be able to recognize the energy objectively.

Let us make this even easier for you and offer to you a list that will assist you to more easily recognize when you are being interfered with. This list is also important as it will help you also see if the intuitive information you are receiving is not of the highest. Here it is:

1. Your information is Money motivated
2. The information stimulates Ego gratification
3. The information feeds a Personal agenda
4. The information contains a Sense of right and wrong
5. The information is in response to a Need for God to appear to you
6. The information is Outside of a sincere love space
7. The information you desire is to Justify a position you feel is right
8. The information you share interferes with another, for example, it Leaves them feeling less than or wrong about their own truth/experience

There is one other critical component to releasing the grip of interference, and it is most important so we state this again. It is:

You are not able to break free from someone else's story
if it is given to you with more passion and energy
than you carry for yourself.

This is a metaphor for the experience of this world. Until you can break free from ALL stories, including past life, and carry enough passion and energy of the truth, you will not ever be able to break free from this illusion.

The astral interferes at this level. It easily infiltrates through your doubt at the level that is seeking passion and energy to know and experience, without the balance of wholeness.

This is why empowering your own heart with discernment is paramount.

One of the keys to unlocking this gift is to be wholly transparent with yourself as you review the list above. And remember, without doubt, The astral will do ANYTHING to gain power through claiming yours.

This is the gift of Ascended Sanity. To fully embrace your truth without doubt and to fully release the need that others must agree with you along the way.

It was over seventy years ago Gandhi stated:

"An error does not become truth by reason of multiplied propagation, nor does truth become error because nobody sees it."

This truth seems as alive in our Ascended Sanity today as it was when it was first shared.

Your Miracle Moment

This message is from the Ascended Masters of Lake Atitlán:
The power of true surrender embraces you all as you navigate a world that seeks to challenge your energetic balance.

To fully surrender is not to give up...indeed it is to embrace the beloved presence within thee without hesitation or resistance. This is the relaxation of divine energy that is simply recognized as a form of surrender.

When you allow the relaxation to enter your energy stream without hesitation, the fullness of your energy is opened to the expansiveness of the universe. To feel any congestion in the body, mind or spirit, simply is the expression of hesitation.

Breathe into your divine expansiveness often and bring forward the joy-filled recognition that you are ready to relax. This is the true surrender.

To embrace this true surrender is to come forward through all illusionary challenges with alert-filled presence. Practice this with conscious attention and from this space, all miracles are manifest as you are the manifest miracle!

Chapter Nine

YOU ARE THE NEW PRIEST

"THE KINGDOM OF GOD DOES NOT COME WITH
YOUR CAREFUL OBSERVATION, NOR WILL PEOPLE
SAY, 'HERE IT IS,' OR 'THERE IT IS,' BECAUSE
THE KINGDOM OF GOD IS WITHIN YOU." [29]

We were on the boat heading out toward TOSA La Laguna again, this time with a distinct difference. For the first time, after two years of consistent dedication, we would at last be staying here. It was an almost surreal moment. Before this day we had only spent hours at a time on this precious land. We had saved numerous beautiful plants during remodeling, walked the ancient Mayan trails and spent time

Sri and Don Maya on the boat shortly after he shared with Sri about the three guardians of the property.

in what we fondly referred to as the "spaceship"—the handcrafted stone Mayan sauna. Yet here, now, this was all becoming real.

As we slept in the new addition that overlooks the small private lagoon, we smiled as we had not fallen asleep to the sound of the waves against the shore before. In the morning, we were acutely aware of the hundreds of hummingbirds and the sounds of other winged creatures. Greeting the rising sun, our heart nearly stands still with every magnificent sunrise across the lake. Yes, this was real, as real as it gets!

On this special morning the high priest was returning. This was a pre-ordained day according to the Mayan calendar—one that had been identified by Don Maya two months earlier. How quickly the time had flown by. It seemed like just yesterday that Don Maya was here at TOSA La Laguna, consecrating what we had instinctively known as an ancient Mayan ceremonial site.

On that day, Don Maya, Amanda and several TOSA community members arrived to offer the first official ceremony at the land. In the late afternoon, Don Maya had arrived from the interior of Guatemala, and Amanda was loudly complaining that it was too close to sunset to do the ceremony. However, Don Maya turned an elder's deaf ear to the complaining and insisted we journey now. This was an auspicious day and we must not let anything stop this ceremony.

It was a wonderful adventure to be in the boat with Don Maya as we got closer and closer to the land. Without any fanfare, Don Maya gazed at Sri, smiled broadly and held up a small smoky quartz crystal. He put the crystal before his eyes as he gazed at the land of TOSA, which was just visible to us now. "There are three very powerful guardians at this place. They are here, here and here," he exclaimed as he pointed to where he saw these mystical guardians.

"This is a very powerful site. I am glad to be here, this is one spot that a very old man has not ever been to, and I am glad I can be here before I leave the planet," shared Don Maya as a simple matter of fact.

Arriving at the shores of TOSA, the sun was already low in the sky, and as we stepped onto the land, both Sri and Amanda tried to

The pile of ceremonial supplies just moments before starting. Note Don Maya's signature pile of hand-rolled cigars.

steer Don Maya to a cleared area close to the shore for the ceremony. After all, it was a beautiful spot, already cleared, and would be convenient for arriving with the heavy boxes of ceremonial supplies.

As Don Maya stepped onto the area that had been suggested for the ceremony, he gazed at Kira Raa, smiled his broad toothless smile and pointed up the path that leads up the steep mountainside. Without any words being exchanged, Kira knew exactly where he wanted to go.

Amanda sighed her discontent loudly as Sri and the others simply acknowledged what we had all known before arriving. He instinctively felt the very site we hiked to each time we visited the land. Our little party grabbed the boxes of supplies and began the steep climb up the mountainside.

Arriving at the rare flat spot that overlooks the lake, Don Maya smiled his approval and immediately took out his large machete to begin clearing the area for ceremony. Although the land was overgrown with vines and greenery, within a fairly short time a perfect ceremonial spot appeared. Once the spot was clear, Don Maya lit one of his famous cigars. It was a tense moment for us all. If his cigar gave the wrong sign, this would not be the spot either.

After what felt like an eternity of watching him puff, look, puff, look, puff, look, we finally were gifted with his dispensation. Yes! Not only was this the perfect site for the ceremony, this was the site for ceremony. He promptly shared that we were standing on the top of the energy of an ancient pyramid and that the ancestor energy of this very spot was delighted we were here and ready to share with us.

We all pitched in eagerly to build the ceremony, which consisted of an extraordinary amount of offerings. There were the usual copal, sugar, corn, chocolate and masses of candles. However, sensing the importance of this ceremony, Don Maya had insisted on many more supplies, including two bottles of vodka to be given to the fire and several bouquets of fresh flowers.

Soon the ceremony was in full celebration, and the fire was speaking loudly. Don Maya was very clear with the final message of this ceremony: *"This is a very powerful spot and it is now being woken up again. Use this spot only for ceremony here and keep it sacred. The healing*

Sri Ram Kaa and TOSA Community members preparing the ceremony at the freshly cleared site.

energy here is very strong and represents the future and the hope of the Maya. You will need to do one more ceremony here on an auspicious day to fully anchor this energy, and I will let you know that day after I consult the Mayan calendar."

The ceremony was a powerful alignment. We entered the timeless space and sense that this gathering of sincere hearts had touched an ancient and powerful vortex of energy. The healing energy of the lake intertwine with the fires of transformation offered us a forceful blessing. We were humbled and close to overwhelmed, and once again, hours had passed. We were on the side of a steep mountain, on a barely passable trail, needing to make our way to the boat dock and then transverse the lake in the dark. It was not an easy task. The ceremony had taken all of Don Maya's energy, and the rest of us were still doing our best to be present with the navigation before us.

With the help of a few dim flashlights, Don Maya climbed onto the back of an agile and eager TOSA community member, who offered to carry him down the trail. The boxes that had held the supplies

The dragon flame has shifted the fire, and the high priest reads the flames.

were loaded with the remnants, and we all started our slow, careful descent in the dark.

Don Maya and a group holding flashlights led the way. Sri, Kira and a helper took up the rear of the procession down the mountain. Taking a brief rest about 100 feet above the boat dock, we heard a large splash in the water and a scream from Amanda. Don Maya had fallen into the lake! He was unable to swim and already weakened from the ceremony, and two of our companions quickly took off shoes and clothes and dove in after him. Rescuing Don Maya and bringing him back onto the shore, we all went to work stripping off his cold, wet clothes and getting him warm. It was still a chilly 20-minute boat ride back to the village, and we needed to do our best to protect his frail health. We held him close during the ride to offer a cocoon of body heat.

Arriving at the house, Don Maya was offered hot soup and a very special healing from Kira and another TOSA community member who was extraordinary at assisting Don Maya to relax into the space of healing. Watching the two work together balancing Don Maya's energy in a harmony of healing love was in itself a beautiful thing to behold. At the end of the session he shared with them: "You heal very differently, and this is the new way. The way of the Maya has been waiting for this. You are here now, and I am now able to go in peace knowing that you have come and will stay."

We tucked him into bed, and realized that the sacrifice of this ceremony had been offered by the elder himself. Aligned with the energy of gratitude and love, the entire group joined together in the large living room, shared and acknowledged the gifts of the day.

Several weeks later, we were waiting for another high priest to arrive to complete the second ceremony that Don Maya had instructed us to create. The chosen day was upon us and our mood was anticipatory. After our first night sleeping at the sacred land, our energy was feeling greatly expanded, and we greeted the arriving boat transporting our high priest and some TOSA community members with bright smiles and joy.

We did not mention where the site was. Nor had this high priest ever been to our land. He stepped onto the land, quickly gazed around, and without any surprise to us, he smiled and pointed his finger up the trail as he nodded yes. All we could do was smile and say "*Si!*"

The sacred site was already calling again! A confirmation of its power and presence.

It was a misty morning, and the rain had come unusually early today. The trail was muddy and the call to presence was important. One false step on the steep trail could mean serious injury. The hike itself felt as if it was part of the ceremony initiating us all into greater presence. As we arrived at the site, the rain began to pour, and we wondered how a fire could ever be made here.

The rain did not exist for the high priest. Arriving at the site, he smiled broadly, offered his approval and began building the ceremony, so quickly we could barely help. The skill and beauty of the ceremony was quite different from the ceremony with Don Maya, yet similarly powerful.

As we all kneeled in the mud and kissed the ground, the energy of the earlier ceremony was still present and we all felt a wave of higher connection swoop into our bodies. Yes, it was raining, but the rain was certainly more than the water from the sky. It felt like a rain of baptism, remembrance and connection.

The fire was rich, and despite the physically smaller size of the ceremonial circle, the fire was almost double the height of the flames from the previous ceremony with Don Maya. The flame played with us, and our high priest stirred the flames, chanted and summoned great energies and presence. At one point the flame looked like a dragon, and we asked if we could break tradition and take a photo of the flame. The high priest agreed.

Once again we were nearing the completion of the ceremony, and the high priest was ready to share with us. "This is a very sacred and

The powerful dragon flame during the ceremony.

ancient site. Deep under the ground here are many artifacts that should not ever be disturbed. Look . . ." he pointed our attention toward the lake. From this site, an energetic flow led directly to the lake.

"This energy is fed by the lake and you," he said, pointing at Kira Raa, "have already seen the city. You have an ancient connection here and this very site will awaken very soon. Anyone who comes to this site with a sincere and open heart can be cured of any illness, any illness. It does not matter if it is mental, physical or spiritual. Here they will be healed. This is powerful land and must be protected. I will help you. We have been waiting for you. It is an important moment for all of our world. Each has different traditions, and I honor that, and when they come here to do ceremony of the Maya, all of those traditions become one, and once again we all become one. It is the way of our future."

The three of us stood in awe and reverence. The high priest had not communicated with Don Maya. He did not know what he had said. He was unaware of the communications that Sri and Kira had with the goddess of the lake or the revelation of the abode of the ascended masters. Yet here was this humble servant of his people, an active high priest, confirming everything that had already been revealed.

In silence we hugged, smiled and collected the supplies for our journey down the muddy trail. The high priest led the way and was eager to share many revelations about the land on the way down. At one point he had his hand on a large rock protruding from the side of the muddy trail. He turned, smiled and looked at Kira as he said plainly, "There is a woman's voice that speaks from this rock. She has much to say, and I would think that you already hear her."

He turned and kept walking. The indigenous people revere *naguals*, natural objects imbued with energy. These naguals are carriers of wisdom passed from generation to generation.

We smiled as he boarded the boat with our companions and they headed back toward the village. Two independent priests, two confirmed acknowledgments of the ancient site and affirmation of the crystalline city. It was almost too much to comprehend in the moment, as we knew there was more to be revealed from this alignment of the ancient wisdom with cosmic truth. Cold, wet and ready for a hot cup of tea, we found ourselves unable to do anything except sit, listen to the waves of the lagoon and integrate the unfolding before us.

※ ※ ※

Many gifts come forward when we allow ourselves to connect beyond the planetary soup or thought body, as easily occurs during these ceremonies. We enter into a world that can only be referred to as divine choice, a powerful realm that we in the developed world often find easier not to dwell in.

For example, let's take a look at prayer. For many, the gift of prayer is a recitation of memorized stanzas created by those who "know better." Often these prayers are in the form of petitions and are designed to overcome our sense of lack of worthiness as the petitioner. "Save us from our plight" is the frequent cry of these prayers.

When we free ourselves to create our own prayer as a means of open connection, the prayer expands. We discover a greater purpose of prayer. We delve into the action of prayer and the miracle of prayer is gifted back to us by taking us beyond the planetary thought body in an extraordinary moment of divine choice in action.

The collective sea of thoughts and energy that surrounds our planet is held here by a magnetism, a gravity that keeps these energies in place. This thought body consists of all the limiting beliefs and emotions of the mass consciousness. If you do not access the cosmic energy that lies beyond the planetary soup, your consciousness will be filled with limiting beliefs and refracted thought forms.

DIVINE CHOICE IS THE SPRINGBOARD OF FREE WILL

What is the reason that we would find ourselves at the moment of divine choice? Can there even be one single reason? And if so, why have we, as the collective of humanity, chosen to bring forward the greatest shift of the ages ever experienced?

Deep within our genetic makeup, an inherently harmonious energy continually seeks to express itself. This expression is one that drives the inner motivation of all actions and can be influenced by either the mind or the heart.

Often, as we expand our life experience, the concept of heart-centered action will appear in one form or another. This can be as basic as empathy for another, and as complex as the mystical spiritual experience. A higher order of heart-centered action can birth through one who encounters a profound life shift.

Through Kira's near-death[30] experience, the gift of absolutely *knowing* that we choose to come to *this* particular planet at this particular moment in a perceived linear timeline offers a recognition of divine choice. In the recognition, an inner shift is available. It was not the near-death experience that created the shift, but rather the release of all doubt as to our infinite being that opened the door to greater freedom.

The word *freedom* is so easily thrown about in our world experience. We seek to be free from constraints that are perceived to interfere with our free will. Constraints range from the young child who feels trapped in school to the frustrated worker who feels shackled to their job. Each experience offers a limited sense of freedom that can become accepted as normal.

We have collectively created a limiting belief system around the experience of freedom. Most people do not want the responsibility that comes with freedom. Thus, structures and institutions have been generated by an intent to support society, yet they actually perpetuate control of the many. The secret agendas of these structures is buried beneath the veneer of freedom messages. While the institutions claim to be serving the individual, in fact they disempower the individual. This causes conflict at the core of our existence. Until you are able to fully let go of the paradigms that hold you captive, you will never be free.

A free people are an empowered people that will not easily be herded, deluded, or unreasonably taxed. True freedom will dismantle centralized power structures.

As you contemplate this, also recognize that true freedom is ultimately the greatest weapon to protect oneself from any system that seeks to control you. It is the fear of your freedom that has given rise to the modern day "pontificators."

You know them as priests,[31] scholars, teachers, scientists, politicians, newscasters, best friends, virtually anyone that is able to persuade you that their opinion is correct. Their opinions and sharing will usurp your clarity to bring forth your own actions and alignments without doubt.

The fascinating piece of this puzzle is that the pontificators have been perfecting their skills for thousands of years alongside the simultaneous perfecting of a society that diminishes self-reliance.

In the earliest Dravidian civilizations (2500–1500 BC), one of the most fascinating revelations from the archeological digs was the marked absence of defined temples. Throughout these wondrous cities, which flourished as merchant and agrarian societies, the only notable religious discoveries were small seals. Some of these seals depicted early deities as nature spirits and also displayed what we now refer to as yogis in seated lotus postures, as seen in the seal below, which many claim is an early seal of Shiva:

What we do know is that when the Aryan invasions came into these societies around 1500 BC, so did the first establishment of the pontificators and class systems. It was with this invasion that the Brahmins were first introduced as the intermediaries who could call forth the pleasure of the gods. They were endowed with great power and their powers, were to first benefit the warriors who were their benefactors.

The obvious divide that has led us to the choices before us now springs from this historical establishment, and regardless of whether you believe in life only existing on this planet or not, regardless of your religious beliefs, your trust in science, and regardless of your personal opinions, this one fact is established:

To facilitate dominion over another, we are trained to willingly give our power to the authority who communes with a higher authority to justify war, conquest and societal norms.

Certainly, at some point you have encountered the statement that more people have died in the name of god than any other reason combined. A simple, thought-provoking recognition that, once digested, forces one to wonder why.

Thoughtfully ask yourself:

• Why have so many people died in the name of god?
• Why do we find it acceptable to die in the name of god?
• How do we reconcile that the primary message of most god-based beliefs is peace and love, yet we justify the slaughter of those who do not agree with a specific point of view?

As you fully digest these questions, notice whether you are experiencing judgments around them. Did you find yourself thinking of one specific religion or belief system? Are you able to simply lift yourself to a place of seeing the bigger picture that is before you? The integrity of the religion was refracted, generating a supportable perspective that is, in fact, in opposition to its teaching.

Ultimately this is the divine choice before us: to see the bigger picture while appreciating the refracted picture. This is a tall task for a species that has become quite adept at giving away personal power and tolerating duplicity.

Taxes and punishment were introduced by the priestly classes in the early part of the fourth century BC to provide security for the kings. We begin to see the direct correlation between the need for safety, a first chakra issue, and the belief that this must be found outside of oneself.

Here is how it all worked. The priests would anoint a king who then offers them protection and wealth as the chosen belief system of the king's society. Then, the king would provide an army to protect this belief system—and the priests—while the people would pay taxes for the protection of this army in case of invasion. Now, of course the people paying the taxes were also the soldiers in the army they were paying taxes to support.

This became the basis of the caste system as established in early India. While many lament the caste system, and despite the outward appearances to the contrary, this system exists everywhere, not just in India, and has also brought us to the moment of divine choice.

Priests, warriors, merchants, servants—these four established categories of human expression are still being acted out today in more refined ways.

The priests, or pontificators, are the perceived authorities, the ones who claim to know the answers, those who have the direct connection. This was first experienced in traditional religion. Today we have gone beyond that, creating the many new religions, or sources of authority, we have come to worship. They may be media-based, politically motivated and health care related. A complex group of priests has arisen to spread the word of their direct communion with the mysterious, whether that is scientific or metaphysical, and we have given them unlimited power due to our fascination with illusion and our addiction to density consciousness.

The warriors are those who implement the will of the pontificators. Well trained in techniques of conquest, they are the favored sons of the priests. Warriors come in a wide variety of forms—world leaders, doctors, lawyers, soldiers, bankers and more. These warriors are carrying out the will of the priests and enjoying the favor of their chosen god for doing so.

This brings us to the merchants, who have come to decide that they did not have what it takes to be warriors or priests. Instead, they worship a different god, a god that provides them with food, shelter, clothing and entertainment. That god is money. As such, it then becomes the merchant's job to serve that god. And through their dedicated service to the god of money, they generate taxes and energetic support for the ruling class.

Merchants do not just own stores. Merchants sell their energy in many forms. They seek an exchange for the "item" of value they have to offer, whether it is a service or an experience of comfort. For them, everything is for sale, and everything has its price. The truth is, everyone at some point experiences their merchant self.

Finally, we turn our gaze toward the servants: the perceived lowest denominator in a system that perpetuates control and restricts freedom. This group of beings has, in essence, freely given up their ability to self-realize. There is a belief that everything that is needed exists outside of themselves. This includes protection, health and security, all to be provided by the system. To trust their own intuition is to create a scenario that they cannot rely upon.

Servants are hiding in all of these perceived structures. Even the most eloquent pontificator can be a servant hiding in the clothing of another—a mouthpiece who charismatically delivers the message of another, a warrior who blindly kills on demand, a merchant who sells simply to sell.

To recognize the further separation from our essential nature through these refracted roles that humanity has adopted over the millennia, is a great step toward unwinding the energies that seek to keep you trapped.

The four classes are not to be fought. The institutions that birthed from these energies need not be the targets for aggression. These classes are the product of the refracted energy within Density Consciousness (see page 60). To become a traditional activist and seek to change society is to perpetuate the refraction by shifting its manifestation. Thus the core energy is not healed. This type of well-intended intervention has brought humanity to the precipice of the ultimate divine choice: *illumination or destruction.*

To be at choice is a celebration. And to break free from the paradigms that are limiting is an extraordinary, though not impossible, task.

Our souls are asking us to take charge. We are being invited to become the new priest! This is the gift of the moment before us and to do so will require a greater sense of nourishment of the soul on all levels of our life experience. After all, if you are the priest. Begin by ministering to yourself.

True nourishment is that which expands balance and harmony, and thus expands true love. True love is all-ways nonjudgmental; it simply radiates an energy of light. For the body, true nourishment offers restorative energy without also delivering a toxic load that must be filtered away in order to find the nutrition. For the soul, true nourishment offers the energy of divine alignment, a restoration of love and light unrefracted by personal agendas.

Understanding Refraction

ARCHANGEL ZADKIEL SPEAKS:[32]

We ask you to release the concept of the individual. It is important for you to understand that the individual was an illusion created to begin with, and through the use of that illusion, it created your separation. Notice how I pronounce that for you. Individ-u-will.

It is not that you do not have your own preference or decision capability, or things that you enjoy while you are here, (on earth). Yet, you are of the one light energy that fractured and splintered.

How can you return to union without first recognizing this?

Understand the blessing of true light has many names and it has greater illuminative ability when we accept that it is many particles that make up a beam. Even the I (Archangel Zadkiel), that speaks to you now is a we.

SRI RAM KAA: The individ-u-will seems to me to be multi layered, meaning, there is the individ-u-will that is owned or identified with from the personality self, the ego. And then there is the actual fracturing of the light and is that not an individuation of sorts?

Ask yourself this question. What am I?

SRI RAM KAA: I am light.

What is light…? Consider it as a spectrum. You have there a clear prism and when the light shines through it what happens?

SRI RAM KAA: It allows the refraction of its component rays.

Correct. You are a refraction; the individ-u-will is on the other side of the refraction. It only exists after the light has hit its body or true spirit.

SRI RAM KAA: Yes. The individ-u-will is light that is on the other side of the barrier which has refracted?

Correct!

SRI RAM KAA: Where is the ego? Is that not a further refraction?

Correct. It would be as if you had this refractory device and you were able to direct the separations into another refractory device that further would separate the beam…Denser and denser and denser. Further and further and further therefore the absolutely last refraction that occurs is when you are here as the individ-u-will. We are all one. Yet, in the one there is oneness.

SRI RAM KAA: Then the travelers[33] are those who can walk through and between the refractory devices.

Yes. How else would you travel? Your mind can understand this if you always think of it as a spectrum. So always think of it as a spectrum.

SRI RAM KAA: Then is there a risk of being lost?

How can you loose that which you are?

*All bound energy is eventually released. It is either released by others who are of a sensory ability to do so while they still are present in physicals. Or they are released at the time of the great release. However, know that all will be released. Understand that through your refracted energy as you ask me this question it implies a perception that once one releases the body the path is done. This is not so. **It is because you are on your path that you are here.***

This experience is simply a part of the overall evolutionary growth of the soul that you are. Individ-u-will is yet another means of growing your light. It is another expression of experience that gives you the opportunity to understand what refraction does. All light is made up of particles of the many. When they refract, the individ-u-will forgets that inside of the light there was every color.

SRI RAM KAA: Such delight.

Yes! It is through this recognition that leads to your expansion; which leads to evolution; which leads one to enlightenment. This is done simultaneously although this is a challenging concept for you here on this planet; to accept that you are in many dimensional realms at once.

SRI RAM KAA: Then must each splinter or fracture become self-recognizing to reunite?

Each fracture, splinter, color or individ-u-will comes to a point where it recognizes it is of highest service to reunite. Only through the recognition, does the reunification begin.

Without recognition there cannot be reunification. One continues in the loop of separateness until each comes to the recognition of the energy of unification. For unification without self-recognition would be a house of cards.

SRI RAM KAA: Yes, really impossible.

Yes. In this manner, a pyramid is built, a planet is built, a world is built, a universe created. Please allow yourself to accept the perfection of the myriad of individuations. You are then able to release judgment of yourself, of those around you, of those you do not even know. Remember that judgment is yet another refractory device, it will further refract the truth therefore making it harder to find because you have many pieces.

Is it easier to put together a child's puzzle that is five big pieces or is it easier to put together the one that is five thousand pieces all looking the similar with subtle differences? Which is easier to complete? For when you apply judgment, know that it is a refractory device and think of it as the complex puzzle.

The moment you remove judgment, automatically many of these pieces bind together, thereby leaving just the few. Both puzzles are solvable, both can be done, one just takes more time. Once either puzzle is put together one can then enjoy its entirety. So the question is how much time do you want to spend putting it back together? So you lay your five thousand-piece puzzle in front of you and remove your judgment and instantaneously it becomes five pieces, and then one.

It is not that they are not both fun and this is important to know. Some may even say "I get more enjoyment out of figuring out these bigger pieces". Or some might say, "I like the challenge of all these little pieces". Is that not symbolic of all lives? Sometimes you enjoy the challenge of the little pieces without even knowing you've chosen complexity. Some might say, "Oh that's too simple: I won't enjoy it".

This is only because they are deep within the struggle and have actually turned it into enjoyment. This is why we give you the analogy of the puzzles.

Model of Refraction of the Individ-u-will

Divine Light is refracted by the Individ-u-will, who continues refracting into ever denser forms of experience.

In third dimensional consciousness, all sense of "reality" is refracted. We adhere to the beliefs that keep us limited and comfortable. Form and density require that we refract the pure light into a vibrational state that is congruent with other density vibrations. To break free of this, we need to heal through the refractions by reclaiming our soul.

At the physical level, healing crisis emerges when the purity of the nourishment is beyond the norm for the individual who is integrating the nourishment. Higher frequency nutrition means that the cells and organs of the physical body must release incompatible elements to make the alignment to the purity.

Similarly, in the emotional body, when higher frequency energies begin to penetrate the auric field around a person, emotional wounds surface for healing. All wounds seek nonjudgmental love to resolve themselves. If the individual is unable to release their own judgments, through forgiveness, then the wounds will not heal. In fact, the ego will put up new psychic armor to support an orientation that inhibits the rapid healing. The metaphor of a healing crisis also applies to our thoughts and subtle bodies.

All beings on earth are in a healing crisis. The energy bathing this planet is a divine dispensation that will propel *all* toward resolution. This universal "energy bath" is heightened when a person is exposed to additional high-frequency experiences and teachings. For example, as we often witness in the days following an Archangelic Insoulment or Avesa workshop,[34] people have their issues stirred. Stuff rises up.

This can be a wonderful accelerator if you are willing to keep pace with the speed at which your soul is ready to guide your evolution. Alternatively it can be destabilizing for an ego which seeks to preserve dominion and control. The ego will preserve unconscious fear and beliefs that it has used to organize psychic and emotional patterns.

Everyone who is integrating energy outside their norm will feel as if they are going crazy. This is because the vibrational structures are not congruent with the existing norm that the ego relies upon for its stability.

The process of authentic spiritual growth requires that the ego step aside and let the soul lead. This can only happen when the ego feels loved and trusts the divine in action at all levels. Authentic evolution is characterized by an increase in the person's vibrational level due to fewer ego refractions.

The popular alternative to authentic evolution is spiritual activism (the second level on the Pyramid of Spiritual Awakening, page 61), characterized by the ego offering more transparency toward spiritual values and finding words and emotions that validate those values. The ego simply offers new structures for approval. Spiritual activism always seeks to control and carries with it a subtle operating system.

How does one break free from spiritual activism? It begins with self-awareness. The emotional body is a density creation and is for the most part governed by the ego. If you have any feelings of hurt, fear or pain, then those feelings are rooted in the paradigms of density consciousness and carry the wounds of the inner child.

Thoughts always arise from feelings. A pain-based emotion will give rise to thoughts to help the brain make sense of the feelings. These thoughts could be defensive or blaming or simply observations.

With a little self-awareness and a dose of willingness, you can choose to heal. You can call to yourself people who will help you release the wounds and limiting beliefs. Without this awareness and willingness to take healthy action, the alternative is to create inner stability by validating judgment and pain. This is done by believing that the cause of the pain is something or someone outside of yourself.

The people of planet earth are indeed in a healing crisis. They are all feeling the energetic shift that is expressing though the disintegration of established structures. The outer world is indeed reflecting that a new recognition is required. We must align our creations more closely with spiritual truth. Integrity with the soul is essential.

As the global reorganization continues, we will most likely witness earth changes, social conflicts and pain within the systems that are contaminated by refracted energy. Those who have not established inner trust with their soul energy will cling to substitutes. The substitutes for the security of the soul are outside authorities, political and religious leaders.

There is no road map in the outer world. The path to unity is a path of love and non-resistance. Your soul knows the way. It is the ego, the inner child and the mind that have lost their way. But the real *You* is not lost. *You* are not frightened. It is time to bring your trust, your identity, closer to the authentic *You*. We have collectively worshipped at the Temple of the Ego long enough. We have received the gifts of its energy, and it is now time for a more authentic teaching.

Of course, the choice is yours. Do you wish to align yourself with teachings and people who offer a temporary "feel-good" experience to the inner child? If so, the world has a wide collection of offering for you, and they are all good. Just recognize that feel-good experiences do nothing but provide a temporary vacation from the inner longing for purity, which is usually experienced as an inner tension.

Do you wish to experience authentic evolution and greater soul alignment? Then chances are, you will have to give up something through a permanent shift in your paradigms! You will be called to give up your attachments to less nourishing activities, people and teachings, even though those parties might be well liked and approved by many. Are you willing to let go of the need for external approval and become the priest of the self?

Within density, every choice will be a negotiation and every relationship a compromise. When the time comes that you say "unplug," the ego will magnetize people and circumstances around you that will test your resolve. You'll then be like the two year old taking a step forward and a step backward, seeking to find your legs in a shaking reality.

The only way through is to hold fast to your spiritual tenacity. To trust the divine more than you trust anything in this world. To be willing to die and lose everything. Then you can break free. No one can do it for you. No group, no religion, no teaching can do this for you. Only you can walk through the creations of limitation that are empowered in your life.

Teachings can remind you of truth and inspire your inner clarity. They can offer strategies for navigating the world. Your soul, however, is the ultimate teacher, the true temple. Will you surrender your agendas and let the soul lead? Are you ready to claim yourself as the new priest?

※ ※ ※

The new priest trusts the divine and knows that their core essence is good. The new priest discovers that gratitude and trust lubricate the hinges of the door to divine guidance. As you empower your energy as the new priest, this one simple practice will fully bring forward the gift of trust and gratitude as a new habit. All it takes is commitment to the simple steps and following through for one month.

THE STICKY NOTES PRACTICE

Supplies needed:
1. One pad of sticky notes (get a kind and color you really enjoy looking at)
2. Pen
3. Commitment to follow through

Step One:

On every sticky note in the pad you selected, write three words:
Thank You—Breathe
The actual practice of simply writing these words on each note brings forward a Zen-like experience and affirmation of the words being written.

Step Two:

Decide where you will place each of the sticky notes on the pad. Get creative. Put one in the glove compartment of your car, or on the flip side of the visor. Open your cereal box and put one inside the lid. Open up a cabinet door and put one there. The possibilities are endless. The key is to find homes for *all* of them.

Step Three:

Commitment time!

Every time you see one of your well-placed notes, do the following:
1. Bring your hand or hands to your heart.
2. Take a deep cleansing breath.
3. Say "Thank you."
4. Smile.

That's it! You will find that if you can commit to one month of this practice you will have literally shifted the way you respond/react to the energy of life. You will also have trained your body to relax and receive your love, a wonderful gift that you are ready to claim.

Your Miracle Moment

This message is from the Ascended Masters of Lake Atitlán:

Our beloved ones in form, navigating a world in body, and a lifetime born into density consciousness, arise and remember who you are! Within your genetic and cellular composition is the deep and recognized awareness of all that is and all that has ever been! Your time of seeking is a chosen one brought forth by your majestic understanding of the great gift of Divine love and presence.

Unwrap your majesty one by one as you breathe and connect to the undeniable truth of your core essence. The majestic presence of your crystalline light shines brightly in all-ways as you empower this energy through your breath and the swirling Merkabah of what you refer to as the head.

Yes, there are many ways of empowerment along your journey and the MOMENT is HERE…NOW…for you to fully call forth the A-Lion-ment of your heart with the full Majesty of Crystalline light. To roar with great and unswerving knowing that YOU ARE as I AM.

Let your eyes once again pour forth liquid light in all aspects of your experience. You may effortlessly remember this gift by simply creating a "crystalline light pool". This pool is found in any large body of water while the sun embraces it. You may also create this by placing clear water in an earthen bowl and placing it into the sun.

When the sun is fully illuminating the water, gaze into the water and see the sun reflected in the water as you connect with the sun into your eyes. Smile and breathe! Then, close your eyes and call forth your A-lion-ment and tone loudly.

All is revealed. All is known. YOU ARE, as I AM.

Chapter Ten

SURVIVING
GLOBAL CHAOS

"WHAT IS THE VEIL? IT IS THE COLLECTIVE
EXPERIENCE OF ENERGY THAT IS RELEASED IN THE
SLOUGHING OF ALL NEGATIVITY THAT IS BROUGHT
FORWARD INTO A PLANETARY THOUGHT BODY."[35]

As we harness the energy of the new priest within ourselves, we more clearly see that many people are unconscious co-creators, lending their energy to refracted visions and embracing trends that have come from outer authorities. People who adopt beliefs without first dialoguing with their own inner authority cement a prison wall around their empowerment and freedom to co-create. Consciousness is the key.

When we surrender to the interpretations of others, we disempower our own divine connection. When we empower fear-based activism through our focus and our money, we subsequently empower the very energy most are trying to release. When we listen to spoken words more than our own hearts, we perpetuate the very disconnect that has damaged the balance in our world.

Yet it is through this process that many awaken. We learn through contrasting experiences, and sometimes we need to embrace an illusion to find our truth. Therefore, we cannot judge the value of an experience. Every experience is contributing to the journey of awakening. Every person is supporting a creation. Are you aware of where your energy goes?

Chaos is a sign of change, a reordering of structures and energies. When we experience chaos, it is a call to find our centers. Within every being is a peaceful calm center. Like the eye of the storm, your inner center is a place of light and clarity. When we organize our attention around outer events, when we reply upon certain conditions to happen in order to feel good about ourselves, chaos is sure to visit us often. At some point you will use the chaos to stimulate a new perspective for yourself.

We are quantum consciousness having a human experience. To the extent we become lost in the human drama, we disconnect from our true power. Like a person wandering in amnesia, we only discover our inner powers when the outer world creates a context that calls them forth.

Many people wait for large life-challenging events to stimulate them into action. Whether a health crisis, a relationship crisis or a career crisis, each outer event mirrors an inner urge to come into greater authenticity. Pain is a cry for union! All pain has its roots in separation. Each time you experience chaos or pain, you have an opportunity to lift your consciousness into closer alignment with your essential truth.

Do you need to create crisis to lift you out of slumber? Or can you simply make a choice to awaken? Are you ready to claim self-responsibility in your daily life? Whether a crisis prompted you into greater alignment or you simply said "enough!" the path requires that each person call back the energy they have invested in egoic patterns and instead invest in authentic expression, no matter how "against the grain" that might feel at first.

Unless one chooses to challenge their automatic patterning with great self-love, unless one focuses their attention on the emergence of divine energy, they will become a victim of the outer world...perhaps in a new, more seductive way. To surrender our ego's domination will not happen unless we feel the unconditional love of the soul. Surrender is not a loss. It is a state of availability to spirit.

And so we travel together, finding allies with whom to enjoy our addiction to density and drama and perhaps to also enjoy our illumined moments. Yet many who start awakening feel an inner foreboding that this too is an illusion. They have no tenacity for setbacks. Thus some may believe that pains of our humanity are inescapable, and that those oasis moments where our needs are fully met are just peak experiences. When one's norm includes existential pain, a sense of lack, one's ego will remain unchecked.

"When one finally moves into acceptance and learns to release fear in a conscious manner, then the subconscious routines of the ego will kick in allowing you the opportunity to further ripen and deepen that acceptance.

In the Illumination of the true remembering, there are trans-neural pathways that will be corrected, unified, and strengthened."

— ARCHANGEL ZADKIEL

The archangels are living energies anchored outside the planetary thought body. As unconditionally loving entities, they are available to offer wisdom and reassurance when called on. We delight in these communions, for the presence of an archangel bathes us in the energy of source.

ARCHANGEL ZADKIEL SPEAKS:

That which you focus on expands; so why the preoccupation with rumination? When you are trapped in self-judgment, the way out is to look beyond yourself. Self-judgment is one of the greatest egoic traps within density. The consciousness of its all about me, is often cleverly disguised as self-deprecating actions and statements, and it does not serve that which you are trying to achieve. **You must learn to look beyond yourself. This is the gift of Divine partnership.**

As you wish to release this part of the ego, as you look beyond yourself, the partner can look beyond themselves, and then the two nourish each other. Look beyond you to your partner. Let your partner look beyond themselves to you. Be wary of the trap of focusing on the ego as being bad! Yes!

We have also discussed compassion, and how when one believes they are being of service, they are often stuck in false compassion. This is the same as self-judgment. You believe that you are doing yourself a service by looking at something that you consider to be less than what you want it to be, which in and of itself is a method of control.

Do you see? It can be most difficult to move out of this trap because the trap in and of itself is self-preserving. So it will mutate like a virus. When a virus discovers that there is something that can get rid of it, it will mutate very quickly to preserve itself. This is what the ego does, this is why the attainment of moving through the layer that you desire to move through can only be done when you remove the focus from yourself. There is no other way to do it in this dimension, for within the density of vessels it is impossible.

SRI RAM KAA: So are you suggesting that any form of self-discipline or self-vigilance is a preoccupation of self and therefore will feed the very thing that you are seeking to dissolve?

It is important to understand that the answer to that question lies in the intent of the vigilance. If you are vigilantly reminding yourself to look beyond yourself, then you will perpetuate a new pattern which will release an old pattern. If, you are vigilant in saying bad ego, go away ego, then that will perpetuate, that which you wish to go away. We are simply expressing to you an opportunity to be in joy.

SRI RAM KAA: I ask because what I am feeling into this day is the absurdity of efforting. I mean I was immersed in letting go of the ego, and in this moment, what I'm immersed in is the recognition to just be.

And what does that mean for you? To just be?

SRI RAM KAA: It means to smile, to smile at my ego, to smile at my Divinity, and to be in allowance and acceptance. We call it nonresistance; to just surrender.

We call it trust. We call it Love. Trust, Love, Trust, Love. When you trust, when you love, the flow is abundant and ever giving of life, and all that you need. Trust that the release is OK, trust that all is in order. Trust it shall be. This efforting is an important venue to look at. For efforting in and of itself is a platform of the ego, is it not?

SRI RAM KAA: Indeed. A spiritual principle that is taught is to focus on making an effort and not focus on the outcome. Basically to center in pure intent, and leave the results to God.

So, simply focus on the intent. What is the intent? Then allow trust, with flow, to provide the how. This is again a trap for you can get into the letting go and trusting, and then do nothing. This is again a very important step to pay attention to.

When one is in trust, one also trusts that there is an action to be taken. It does not imply that I should sit and wait and a phone will ring with my answer. Trust means that you trust yourself in the steps you are taking. You trust the action you are being guided to do and you use as your barometer the degree of joy and fulfillment and nourishment that comes from the action you are taking. You trust that if it is not there, then there is a new direction that is provided, even if it is not one you want to create, even if it does not look like that which you believe it should look like. That is the way to do it.

There have been many who we hear all the time begging, help me, help me, yet they do not step into their own flow. They do not step into the action. We are helping, we are always there. Yet, if you do not reach out, how can we assist? This is the trust, the great trust and love of the self enough to do the action you are guided to do, and to truly honor the barometer of joy. Understand that joy is a state of being not an emotion. This is an important distinction. When many hear the word *joy,* they assume it means giddy or laughter. *Joy is peace. Joy is love.*

Joy is a state of being. It is a way of living where you are in compete acknowledgement and harmony with your authentic being. *You are able to relax into trust so implicitly there is not one second spent on the double asking.* When you truly flow from one action to another without questioning, that is when you know. When you stop with the second guessing of yourself, your actions, your being-ness; when you simply stop questioning what are you doing. This does not imply recklessness, it implies complete peace, trust, flow, and knowing. Balanced in that recognition is of course quiet time, a time of reflection, and the time to receive guidance for which you can act upon.

The concept of meditation has become convoluted on this planet. **Meditation is any process of sincere intent directed toward achieving inspired guidance.** Many ask, "How do I know it is inspired? How do I know it is true guidance?" There is only one answer.

Does it give you greater joy? Does it provide a sense of love? Do you feel peace?

If anything you receive in quiet reflection causes you distress, make sure you understood correctly. **True universal energy will only create feelings of Peace, Love and Joy.** This is the most simple and direct barometer we can offer anyone. It is also important to remember that meditation takes many forms. Perhaps it also needs to have many definitions. We may refer to it as meditation, you may call it reflection, inspiration, quiet time, it does not matter.

However, when your entire being **is** meditation, when your existence is meditation; that is when the questions you ask are no longer even in your thought process to ask or even to formulate. This is a barometer. Now we encourage you to be careful as you listen to these words for they can trigger a loop of self-judgment. This judgment may wish to express itself as the belief that you are not doing enough now. Remember, the very trigger that sends that message to you is the same one that knows you are already doing everything you need to do.

It is all meditation. It is all joy. Trust, do not second guess. Presence is love, love is trust. Trust gives presence.

Presence is love, love is trust.
Trust gives presence.

Presence

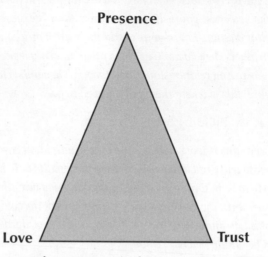

Love   **Trust**

For you must have presence in the present. Otherwise it is a false symptom of one who is on a path of aspiration. OK, I'm present, now.... *now what? You must have your presence in the present. Always remember this.* **Your presence honors divine light through the recognition that trust and love are inseparable.** *Trust is love and love is trust, and let it begin with you.*

If you find yourself unable to begin with you, then this is when you are being called to go beyond the you ever more; to claim your presence, in the present.

SRI RAM KAA: The present is the presence.

Yes, that is correct and it must begin with you. For you see, when you are able to bring your presence into every breathing moment, then you are unshakable. You are then so connected, so available to yourself, that there is not an event that can ever stop you from your Divine connection. This is not to say that there would not be momentary connection with the pain of events, for the pain of the pain is the habit of this sphere. However these moments are fleeting and will shift in their ability to affect you in a manner that is now different.

169

They shift because they love you. Yes, you have shifted because you love you. We love you. You are love, so therefore you know love, therefore you become love, therefore you are the presence of love, which also means you trust yourself, your partner, your life, yes!

Within relationship in your world there are many couples do not trust each other. They do not trust each other on many levels, this is the number one reason relationships do not work. They must claim Divine Partnership, this is where they will all need to go.

SRI RAM KAA: Building trust?

Yes, however this is work that is done on an individual basis first. You must come to trust and love yourself unconditionally; only then are you truly ready to be in Divine Sacred Union. You may be with the correct partner, yet until the veil of distrust is lifted, until the comprehension that trust is love and love is trust is looked at, acknowledged and owned, it cannot be Divine Sacred Union.

You honor God when you honor yourself.

Now is a good time for humanity to cast off limiting beliefs and empower authenticity.

For those of you who experience regular disappointment or depression or anxiety and have self-doubt as a frequent visitor in your consciousness, please consider this: you are addicted to pain. Pain is as addictive as drugs and alcohol. Pain narrows your point of view, clouds your clarity and motivates behaviors that are not in the highest self-interest. Pain offers a continuity of energy to the ego; it is an addiction!

How does one stop an addiction? First recognize that you are addicted. Then look at the payoffs for being deluded versus the payoffs for awakening. Then make a choice. It will be hard regardless of what you choose. It is hard to live a life in pain and struggle. It is hard to break free from the pattern of pain-based living and find your freedom. But the moment you break free you will celebrate all that you have every experienced and you will find joy in you past pain. If you choose to slumber instead of awaken, celebrate that choice. Know that when you are ready, really ready, you will make a new choice.

True joy is always present, even in the pain. Once you can see the joy, the pain will subside. That is the paradox of clarity: celebrating the delusion that we feel trapped within actually frees us from the compulsion to stay in prison! The shift begins by smiling at your pain...look at it and smile.

Humanity is now heavily addicted to pain and fear. No amount of bargaining, no brilliant strategizing, new officials or conferences will resolve the problem. Governments are reactive. Science is retrospective, and people in pain are too distracted by the drama and immediacy of their problems to see that they can simply say "enough" and stop the drama.

Yes, the pain will end when you say, "I've had enough. I get it. I am the creator of this suffering." That recognition alone parts the chaos for a moment where you can empower authentic choice. Yet, it will not carry you fully out of the prison. The first step is recognition; the second step is to take action, and don't look back! The energy released by the "Ah-haa moment" is like candy for the ego, and while this Ah-haa can indeed shift your life circumstance, it can also launch a new challenge for you. That challenge is learning to discern the rise of the spiritualized ego.

Each release from the density delusion unleashes your quantum power. As your consciousness comes more closely into alignment with your core essence, authenticity radiates. A charisma radiates around you. This empowers your own Divine Attractor Belt, and life's blessings seem to pour your way.

Co-creation is not a special power given to the masters. It is given to all. It is the very fabric of your existence. You are a creator, and the universe is creation. You dance in the creation and thus play in a greatly mirrored playground. As the brilliant creator, you have done a brilliant job of seducing yourself into believing that you are limited, mortal and vulnerable.

The earth and its inhabitants are collectively headed toward great reconstruction, a transformation of form. We are at a profound moment where most everyone can agree that the need for transformation is irrevocable. It is HOW we move through this process that integrates and encompasses our free will.

Density consciousness embraces the limitations of the gameboard. This level of consciousness has generated all the joys and all the problems we witness in our three-dimensional world. While we honor and respect density consciousness as the first step in the evolution of self-aware beings, it's really just kindergarten. Now it is time to graduate. The universe has sent us the signal that we must release this level of consciousness.

- Are you ready to lift off the gameboard of earth school?
- Have you played long enough in density consciousness?
- Are you ready to accept your co-creative power?

These are not simple questions. A firm and committed "yes" to any question will bring forth some form of chaos in your life because everything will shift. A change in consciousness affects everything. Growth is feared as death to the ego because each growth experience brings about new rules. Lifting into ascension awareness is opening the door to your quantum beingness, and the ego cannot preserve its domain if you really anchor there. Mystics talk of a "dark night" and "dying to oneself"—common pathways for those who have the courage to face their deepest fears.

To lift off the gameboard and empower one's true mastery is a path of enlightenment. It requires focus and tenacity. We know and live this choice as the path of Self-Ascension.

It is our knowing that *all* beings on this planet can Self-Ascend into their authentic alignment, into their true fearless mastery, which is what some refer to as the higher self. The question is, *When* will they choose to fully awaken to their authentic truth?

When any "one" awakens, it is a choice. It is the ascended individual's job to simply hold the space of love for others. Thus we midwife each other into an ever-refining expression of purity.

Each step of the way, new revelations become understood and we view the process differently than before. Thus, with commitment to our essence, we learn to release all forms of attachment. As we walk through the process, we learn that attachments, especially inner attachments to judgments and beliefs, limit our Joy and constrict the creative flow.

❋ ❋ ❋

THE RESURRECTION OF SELF-ASCENSION

"I am the Resurrection and the Life!"
—JESUS, THE CHRIST

ARCHANGEL ZADKIEL SPEAKS:

Now is the time of Great Resurrection. This lesson is about the true meaning of resurrection and the disparities among the definitions of this word in your world.

What is resurrection? Why do many fixate upon it? Why do many become so preoccupied with resurrection? Who was Jesus, and why did he resurrect?

In the understanding of the Self-Ascension process, resurrection is a term that does not have a separate meaning from Self-Ascension. They are very much one and the same. From the moment you are born into this expression of density you are resurrecting.

Understanding what this means has a far broader scope than, "Let me kill you and see if you rise from the dead...oh, you did...resurrection." No, it is much broader than that, for that is a density based limited view...very limited.

The perspective of resurrection we offer is the same as Self-Ascension. In terms of resurrection, when you remove yourselves from the light, when you become refracted pieces that move further and further into density away from light, then symbolically this is death, a separation from source energy. The resurrection process begins the moment your path is determined and you arrive on this world.

This applies to all lifetimes, as all experiences are part of what is now the culminating resurrection of all Divine Light. When you arrive here, in this form of density, you are already in your resurrection process, although you may not feel it, know it, or even be aware of it. And so, you begin the process of Self-Ascension/resurrection.

Once you begin this process, all of your energetic experiences are carried forth and contained in each and every lifetime, regardless of where it may have occurred. It is important to remove the limited view that all lifetimes occur on this planet, or even in this galaxy or dimension.

*Yes, there are those beings that are bound to this planet, so all of their lifetimes are on this sphere. This is what you must understand. If you are bound to this planet or any other for all of your lifetimes until completion, it was by your choice. **All incarnations are by choice.***

There are some who make a different choice with each incarnation, and there are some who make one choice initially and then have all their incarnation experiences within that one choice.

*As you re-collect your energetic **expansionism** through every experience of your refracted particles, it contributes to the resurrection of the reunification that removes refractory devices and brings all beings back to wholeness. It is most challenging to explain this so that the mind of this world comprehends, and so we do our best.*

It was many refractory devices that further and further created the Individ-u-will that brought you through all of theses different lifetimes. (see Figure-A) They are now being gently and systematically removed. For if they were all removed in an instant, the collective shock would create a wave of energy that would throw the sensitive balance of life energy into imbalance. So from out of respect for the mind, it must be done in a gentle manner.

Every event, every energetic shift that occurs on this sphere here, affects all other dimensions simultaneously. It is as if you take calm water and drop something heavy into the water and big ripples go out. This is the effect you all have throughout the universe.

The Universal Effect

If you take calm water and drop something heavy
into the water big ripples go out.
This is the effect you all have throughout the universe.

Because of the immense power of the shift and the effect of the shift, it must be done in accordance with vibrational harmony. This is why all events seem to have a time and a place as you say. This is not to say that something happens according the linear time line of your world, however it does occur within the Divine order of expansion. The evolution of the energy has come to a point now where it is ready to be reunited. With the removal of each refractory device, you start the integration process.

This is why it is a joyous time! It is as if an explorer has discovered the new world and has successfully explored that world without creating damage to that which it has been exploring. The explorer has filled their ship with all that was offered to go and is ready to return home successful!

The greatest gifts of all of your incarnations are ready to reassemble. Is that not truly resurrection? How could resurrection simply be for one person, one being? Why must it require a violent act? This is the paradigm that many get stuck in on this planet. Many energies *are expressed with violent graphic detail to shock the psyche into belief patterns and then to hold that belief system through fear.*

This system of conditioned belief patterns is a big concept to embrace and then to release. When you understand true resurrection, you understand that it is also Self-Ascension. As each Self, ascends, it becomes part of the great resurrection of all! Thereby it does not diminish the importance of each Self ascending, it further gives the proper perspective of the joyous gift of Self-Ascension for you are being of service to all. Through your many incarnations you are coming closer to assist with lifting all of the refractory devices and coming back into the compete recognition and the joy of union on all levels.

SRI RAM KAA: So, you are saying that Self-Ascension is contributing to the removal of the refractory devices, and the coming mass event is not significant enough dimensionally to cause any disruption, yet it may look like disruption to those who are still anchored within the individ-u-will?

Correct, which is why many beings from many dimensions are communicating with your planet in many ways, it is a means of offering the energy that supports you to Self-Ascend. Thereby as with all events, it occurs within the vibration of balance. Without balance then you would have that heavy object dropped into water. This is why it is not a surprise that so many are becoming aware that the shift or the rift in the shift is becoming greater…polarization is increasing…which is simply creating balance.

However, at the current time on your planet there are more who are polarized in fear than are not. This is why we are here…to support all light bearers and to assist in providing the energy for all who wish to claim it, that have chosen the self-ascension process.

SRI RAM KAA: So awakening others to the choice they have already made is part of this teaching, and providing that support for them.

It is important to honor all definitions of all words, however for the purpose of great service in the time of the great resurrection, it is good to express the broader view, to recognize that each individ-u-will self-ascension contributes to mass ascension which leads to the removal of

the refractory disturbances and enhances re-unification with the one
God of connection, light, love, and peace.

We wish you great awakening as your world has entered the time.
It is a new phase, and the energy has now come in and will continue to
be integrating. Understand that a new phase of all life has begun. You
are loved, you are supported, and we are always with you.

※ ※ ※

To co-create a new world experience requires that we access a level of creation outside the stream of consciousness that is supporting the conflict and destruction in our world. This is *not* about adopting a new set of values or installing some sort of laws or police force to insure peace. It *is* about resolving your own state of being that could ever participate in conflict. This means bringing the light of love to the human shadow. The shadow is not your enemy; it is an aspect of consciousness guarded by the human ego.

A great degree of lift can be realized as we do our inner healing work. A greater degree of lift can be enjoyed as we forgive others and ourselves and move past the need to judge another being. A great degree of lift can be enjoyed if we bring our focus toward the beauty in the world, as we start looking for the Divine in all things. Further lift is realized as we allow gratitude to be the pivotal energy of our interactions.

All relationships—whether with people or other participants in our experience—are there for your good. Assume an attitude of gratitude and the gift offered through the interactions will become conscious. It is your energy that quiets the chaos around you.

Gathering mystical revelations directly from the Mayan high priests, in synergy with the archangelic realm and in harmony with divine universal wisdom, we have unlocked many keys to navigating these times. Yet these keys are not understood by the mind of density. Thus the paradox of spiritual evolution continues. The practices we share in this book can help you experience your essential nature if undertaken with sincerity. The are countless other practices that can help, but none will ever truly work for you if you carry the energy of a seeker.

Being a spiritual seeker is a fine first step, yet it will always fall short of the goal, for a seeker never finds. Instead, the energy of a *finder* is closer to the truth of ascended consciousness . . . but not quite. For the nature of true beingness is that there is nothing to find. Nothing is lost! It's silly to write about enlightenment. What is useful is to touch the energy of truth in your own being and let it guide you.

We invite you to experience this anchored presence and remember without doubt why you are on this planet at this very moment in history. The time of simply talking about unity and praying for unity has passed. These are wonderful methods that have prepared us to simply claim the divine synergy that is now ready to fully come forward onto our planet now.

We are rapidly approaching a moment where we can come together collectively and stand in our integrity as one heart declaring to the universe that we are awake, that we are responsible co-creators and that we are ready to bring the gift of this divine energy to our planet!

It all begins with a sincere willingness: willingness to let our soul lead, willingness to let go of our need to control, a willingness to trust change, a willingness to relax into our ascended hearts. This does require some practice, for we must interrupt the states of consciousness that reacts to the storms around us and instead midwife ourselves into a higher expression of being. Our mastery will not be turned on unless we claim it.

☀ ☀ ☀

A Spiritual Practice to Transcend Chaos

Let us first remember that the purpose of a Spiritual Practice is to re-connect with the truth of your Being. Authentic Spiritual practices offer an alignment with our Soul that is restorative and nourishing.

Most people seek a sense of internal peace. Many people seek guidance and reassurance on their journey of discovering this peace. They often use spiritual practices to help modulate the stress of day to day living. This is certainly useful, yet, for many, these practices are simply coping mechanisms.

The higher purpose of problems is to awaken your inner resources and expand your wisdom. To simply cope better with the chaos and the pressures of the world empowers and perpetuates that very process that caused the stress in the first place! Simply stated, are you organized around your problems or are you organizing your consciousness around your Enlightenment?

The density mind had been trained to create endless complications. The ego can find countless density attachments. At some point, the authentic You that is in the body, will step forward and remind itself that you have done all this before. At some point each person decides it is time to lift into a new frequency.

The following spiritual practice is very simple and very powerful. It will delight you with its ability to immediately stop density chaos. The more you practice this experience, the more frequently and effortlessly you will enter multi-dimensional space in ways that the mind can not understand. Remember, your soul knows the way!

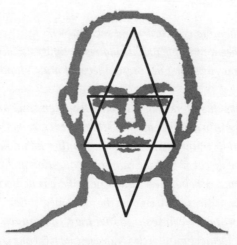

Look into a mirror at your facial structure. Now, mentally draw the two pyramids, using your own face as your guide to your sacred geometry. You might even want to draw the merkabah on the mirror in order to help you visualize this sacred geometry, (A sharpie pen works great!)

Understanding the Merkabah of the Face

Each one of us carries our own sacred geometry. It is expressed through our bodies. Let us become reacquainted through working with the Merkabah of the

Face. A Merkabah is the shape that is formed by two intersecting pyramids, one pointing up and the other pointing down.

On your face, the downward pointing pyramid begins at a line drawn through the center of the eyes and continues downward, following the natural geometry of the outside the mouth to the base of the neck, terminating at the throat chakra.

The upward pointing pyramid begins at a base line formed at the center of the mouth and continues upward as it passes through the center of the eyes to the top of the forehead (see illustration).

The activated Merkabah will open interdimensional space and offer alignment with Soul wisdom that is beyond this world. There is one catch, however, this can be done only when you are centered in your heart and willing to accept your authenticity.

Divine wisdom will not be accepted or even recognized if one is afraid. Are you addicted to your density world view? The Merkabah of the Face opens a cosmic connection that transcends religions and world views.

Bring your hand to your heart and ask yourself:
• Is there a place within me that would resist understanding?
• Do I wish you go beyond my present level of understanding?

Each of us has this Merkabah of Divine Transcendence available to lift our consciousness into a higher alignment. However, sometimes the mind blocks our evolution through incessant questioning and doubting. As we relax the mind we discover that we can **be** the question and we can **be** the answer. As we practice being-ness we discover there is no need to question; we simply live the answers. We become the awakened state.

Ask the Heart to come forward so that the mind can relax. You might even command: "Dearest mind, relax...dearest heart, **take over!**"

Each of us is awake to the level of consciousness that brings us comfort. Relax your mind. Breathe deeply and fully, open your heart and trust yourself. Self-trust opens the doorway to your authentic evolution.

Activating Your Merkabah of the Face

Sit comfortably with your spine as straight as possible. You can also lie down. It is useful to breathe deeply, drawing the breath up from the base of the spine as golden streams of purifying light.

Place the middle finger of one hand at the base of the throat and the center finger of the other hand at the top of the forehead, at the hairline. Feel, sense, and see the intersecting pyramids. Breathe again.

Close your eyes and feel those two fingers at the tips of the intersecting pyramids. One pyramid has its base at the eyes and the other pyramid has its base at the mouth.

Activate the Merkabah further through your relaxed presence. Allow your heart to expand, send golden light up the spine. Simply holding this posture and focus will be very centering. When you are ready, simultaneously then pull your hands out to the side and spin the Merkabah.

To spin the Merkabah is to open a portal of Beingness that will ignite your Authenticity. As you practice spinning the Merkabah, you may discover that the top pyramid spins one direction while the bottom pyramid spins in the opposite direction. You may find that sometimes you will be guided to have both the top and the bottom spin the same direction. Practice this. Trust yourself. Your soul knows the way.

Your Miracle Moment

This Message is from The Benevolent Ones:

With a smile of broad delight we offer thee the glorious momentum of eternal light expanding now through your heart and your being.

As your Essene heart stabilizes and anchors the unification of healer, brother, sister, mother, father, daughter, son and friend, you open up to the ancient and yet over present energies of the truth of your soul.

As an expression of Divine presence you have embodied all roles. As an awakened being of Divine love you integrate all these roles into the moment by moment expression of presence in form.

To embrace the formless form while enjoying the expression of a body is to fully offer the gift of healing to yourself and to your companions on your planet of choice. This is the essence of all healing...to fully lift into the formless expression while still experiencing form. To embrace the joy of Divine presence while offering Divine love. To celebrate this gift without feeling that your work is now done. Is this not a great miracle?

For when you fully step into this anchorship, you dissolve the remaining remnants as if they had never existed, and the smile of eternity joins again with those who are already smiling, and you discover you are and have all-ways been ... free!

Chapter Eleven

ΠΑΥΑΠ SUΠRΙSE

We have spent many weeks in the highlands of Guatemala at the request of the Mayan high priests and elders. While many still do not wish to have their most sacred mysteries revealed, those with great visioning capability recognize we are at the moment of reunification. The Mayan elders are confident and prepared for an imminent shift into the age of light.

Sri asked an elder, "What is the impact of the reunion of the Eagle and the Condor?" His reply was, "More light!" Then Sri asked, "What about the cycle of the ages coming in 2012?" The elder's eye twinkled as he looked deeply into Sri's eyes, "It means even more light," he replied!

Throughout our journeys deep into the highlands, we have discovered that the Maya live in the ultimate dream world. This is a powerful discernment as it is not the dream of illusion. What it is demonstrates the collective dream of creation and co-creation. How we harness this creative potential to call forth the dream is the gift before us all now.

At the center of the expression of the highland Maya, they create through their weavings, stories, tribal living and constancy of being. Through the ancient arts of backstrap weaving, hand-hewn canoes, and the creation of all that surrounds them, every moment is the embodiment of the fullest aspect of Maya.

While many of the younger Maya go to school and learn Spanish, the native languages are making a form of revival amongst the tribes. During the civil war of recent years, as well as during the times of conquest, to speak the native language was akin to a death certificate.

We have experienced the languages of Cakchiquel and Quiché. These languages are complex to pronounce, as is evidenced by the belly laughs of those who have tried to teach us. Mayan languages call forth great symbolism and are filled with rich heritage.

On the same day that Kira was speaking with Mariana about the menus and the cooking, earlier that morning she had introduced Kira to her daughter with great pride saying, "Kira! Angelica speaks perfect Cakchiquel. She is so smart."

There was a broad smile on her face as Angelica looked up at Kira, feeling the gift of her mother's pride. Then, Mariana went on to say, "I do not speak Cakchiquel because my mother was afraid to teach me. But, I make sure my daughter knows how!"

In a beautiful way, this simple task, feeling that it is now safe to teach children the language of their heritage, is a sunrise for the Maya. It is the authentic recognition that we can resurrect ourselves at any moment when we are clear, focused and committed.

The Mayan sunrise that is upon us all is the return of the collective dream. It is the return of our natural and harmonious ability to connect with the essential. Within us is the recognition that we can bring forth the elements of creation to a full and resurrected experience without the energy of victimization.

If we gaze at our conditioned understanding of the word *Maya*, it first calls forth the definition of the people of Mesoamerica. Any

Mayan gardener Alejandro joins Sri at TOSA La Laguna to lend his beauty to the lakeside retreat. Alejandro laughs with Sri and Kira that he speaks as little Spanish as they do, therefore they understand each other perfectly. He arrives each day from the village in his handmade canoe and gently glides it home when the sun begins to set.

185

quick web search will reveal this. If you decide to look deeper, you will begin to discover that there are several Vedic or Hindu understandings of this word, the most poignant being:

The power of a god or demon to transform a concept into an element of the sensible world.

This is an important definition to consider at the moment of a Mayan Sunrise: *the power of a God or demon to transform.* The choices before us are indeed just that. The higher aspects of man have acted as the gods, transforming our world and our future. Similarly, the lower aspects of humanity have brought forth their own transformations in what could easily be viewed as a demonic expression of creative forces.

As our world lives through its own dark night of the soul, we have the opportunity to heal separation and burst forth from the chaos as a unified presence. This healing recognizes that all paths are valid. All paths lead us home to our soul.

Reunification of the Eagle and the Condor is a symbolic vision that bridges many expressions of separation. The reunification creates the rainbow bridge of light anchored by the heart and sustained by releasing doubt directed toward ourselves and our universe. To fully enter the age of light, we must become this unified energy. Words do not make this happen. Speeches and books do not create the golden era.

We have seen that ideas launched from density consciousness will not offer the level of healing our world is calling for. We are past the time where rearranging the pieces on the game board would offer freedom to the players. It is our presence that will free others to find their ascended hearts. The next level of conscious is known by its presence, its light. Ascended presence through ascension consciousness frees our minds and expands our hearts, and authenticity emerges without doubt or fear for our future.

If there is to be a golden era, it will not be ushered in by the mainstream. This is an impossibility, as the mainstream is anchored upon the density consciousness that has supported victim consciousness and built social programs around it. Density actually embraces the disconnect between mind and heart, allowing domination and pain, and isolation of global resources into the hands of a few. Only density consciousness can tolerate offering high-ideals in words and ignore horrid behaviors from the very institutions that espouse the high ideals. We offer this as a reminder, not a criticism.

We have all co-created density. There are joys and a great value in this level of consciousness. However, it is not our final destination! Density consciousness is like the taxi driver who rushes the pregnant woman to the hospital to give birth. He (density) has offered a great service. Are you ready to get out of the cab?

Consciousness is fluid; it is a self-aware entity. Like an ocean, it can suspend both garbage and brilliant light. As humanity rises through density consciousness into spiritual activism, many are touched by the purity of the higher levels of being. Many are touched by the great inspiration that is available, the great love and connection.

Being touched by these frequencies offers a wider perspective, the opportunity to discern where we all are. By enlarging the canvas of our experience to include the seeming mystical realms of being, we have the opportunity to recognize the fabric of co-creation. In the recognition is the freedom. Remember, the first step of empowerment is conscious recognition… and the next step is taking action!

The golden era will be ushered in by small groups of people who hold ascension consciousness. That is, these people have fully unplugged from the hypnotic magnetism of density consciousness, thus the masses may not fully understand these groups. Yet the love and harmony expressed between members of these small groups will communicate a sincerity that touches those who choose to look deeply.

All human beings radiate energy based upon their level of consciousness. The collective thought body that surrounds the earth is comprised of all the fear-based thoughts and all the harmonious thoughts. Each radiates an energy. We know that love-based thoughts offer a harmonic that offsets many lower frequency emanations. That is, the higher frequencies are more forceful than the coarser frequencies.

Archangel Zadkiel has often shared with us that one person anchoring in the ascended frequencies liberates 100,000 others to also remember who they are. A small group of light workers who gather together without an egoic agenda send out a wave of healing energy that will offset the discord of a small city—an extraordinary use of harmonic energy.

If this sounds fantastic to you, check into the research done 20 years ago by the Transcendental Meditation Institution. They demonstrated that when meditators gathered as a group in a city, holding the energy of peace, the crime rates lowered. This was statistically demonstrated. The challenge is living full-time in that state, not just holding that level of consciousness for a few hours.[36]

Gather with like-minded friends and practice. Support each other to lift from habitual thoughts and embrace the revelatory wisdom that will come through introspection. Sing and move together. Share from your heart and allow yourself to be free to love and be loved. The new communities will be aligned with holistic practices, incorporating the meditative state into action and song.

Authentic leadership inspires authenticity, not followers. True leadership is a model, a demonstration of authenticity. Being in the presence of an authentic leader awakens your own ascended heart wisdom and stimulates your empowerment. Authentic leadership inspires alignment. To align with another, to align with a teaching or a vision, affirms that you see the truth of the vision. Being aligned does not ask you to give over your personal authority to another. It is a statement of congruence.

The density model of leadership requires followers. The leader, like the priests of old, are granted authority over their followers, as if their wisdom was superior to yours.

Wisdom is not a commodity. It is a recognition. A teacher inspires in a student the recognition of truth. The truth then is felt, seen and known by the student and the gift of the teaching is now held in both student and teacher. There is no hierarchy; there is a mutual recognition of truth.

Consciousness is fluid and ever-expanding. There will be those who anchor at different frequencies along the spectrum, serving as torch bearers for others who are traveling the path of Self-Ascension.

The universe is infinitely patient. Those who wish to dwell longer in density consciousness can indeed choose that arena. Those who feel the call of awakening need support, for density is the arena of manipulation and domination. Those who want to awaken appear as threats to the ego-driven world. Thus density will do its best to seduce you, to call you back into its slumber so that you might lend your co-creative energy into that ocean of disconnect.

If your heart is stirred and you feel that you are awakening from a dream, honor yourself. Go inward and cultivate your discernment filter. The forest is filled with the trees of density. Some are quite beautiful. Seek not the fruit that falls from those trees. Instead, admire the beauty and then keep walking. If you stop and partake of the fruit of density, you will slumber. The good news is that at some point you will again awaken to the stirring inside, and then the journey of awakening begins anew.

The Maya, like other indigenous peoples of the Americas, have been persecuted and separated from the mainstream. The children of these people, confused by the power structures of the new ways, become disconnected from their authentic roots. While the indigenous high priests and elders still practice the old ceremonies and beliefs, for many of the youth, their heart has been given to the mainstream's promises. They want the fruits of density; their ego has been seduced. They are at the moment of their own resurrection, of remembering what it is to be Maya.

To align with the earth's wisdom is to be a partner with Gaia. To recognize her authenticity and to honor balance and sustainability are imperative wisdoms to be embraced. Remember, alignment is the act of an empowered partnership.

The Maya live in small groups with the values of a village. Their alignment with agriculture has taught them that many hands indeed lighten the load on the individual. Yet, they never created cities of millions. Instead, new groups branched off and new cities were formed. This is native intelligence.

Today millions occupy a city and as a result have disconnected even further from natural cycles. Big cities become dependent upon resources that are located far away. The cycles of day and night are distorted and the crowding of the people collapses individual energy fields. As a result of the energetic collapse, people in cities are more susceptible to illness, fear and manipulation by outside forces.

In the times ahead, those who live in the cities will be impacted severely. They will be among the first to taste the fruits of negative trends. This can appear as food shortages, power outages or even martial law. Those who live in large cities will find that their sense of safety and well-being will come through organizing themselves into neighborhoods and caring for each other.

In short, a return to village life, of any form, will be the healthy response to the harsh conditions ahead. When was the last time you grew a vegetable? Even a city window makes a perfect garden.

We do not suggest that people must emulate the Maya or any other tribe. We do suggest that you pay attention. The aboriginals on every continent, along with other traditions that are rooted in ancient knowing, all have gifts to offer. There are seeds of light in them all.

Ancient civilizations are not our future, yet they have shown it to us. We honor those who have gone before us. We accept the wisdom of the ages, for it is part of us already. Past lives and ancient tribes are just that: *past*. We have already lived those stories. Every past accomplishment is stored in our collective DNA. We do not need to dig up an ancient city to find truth. But we may need to touch a relic in order to reconnect with an ancient wisdom hidden within ourselves.

Therein is the difference. In the return to unity, each will touch the ancestral worlds just enough to cultivate respect and remembering. In the respect is the empowerment of authentic freedom. True respect is a state of consciousness that recognizes the gifts and witnesses the truth of another. There is no need to bow, yet in the bowing is an honoring of the divine energy that was and is acting through them.

Bow to all and bow to yourself. The divine wisdom is ever-present, awaiting your recognition. Celebrate consciousness. Celebrate your own ever-widening understandings. Celebrate the creation energy that has supported us all to have the life experiences we require to awaken.

The Maya have honored us by allowing us to touch their deepest wisdom. The Maya have, perhaps unwittingly, allowed us to use them as a vehicle of our own awakening. And, in the awakening we recognize that Central America was one of the initial seeding points for life on earth. Returning to the place of our birth, we find resolution, a sense of completion.

Awakening is truly a continuous celebration, for the Joy keeps getting brighter! With our clarity, focus and commitment, we gather in the recognition that we are free.

The authentic Maya consider themselves to be children of light. Perhaps we are all Maya.

Now is the time.

Are you ready to call forth your Mayan Sunrise?

Are you ready to co-create a Mayan Sunrise for our planet?

Your Miracle Moment

This culminating message is from the Benevolent Ones!

Greetings dear ones of the world of the blue sky. We come to thee today to share with you the miracle of the Divine Presence that is now coming forth with great momentum.

As the ocean sends waves to shore that disintegrate and then go back out to the ocean to begin again, so your world is now the wave that is close to shore.

For millennia you have been building momentum and energy to fully come forth as a powerful source of Divine presence, and so you are ready. What does this mean to encompass your world with the energy of Divine presence?

It offers to each and every being the gift of Knowing their true nature without hesitation, thereby calling forth ALL THE RESOURCES of the Universe to fully co-create in harmony with the planet and all beings.

When the gathering of those who have chosen to empower Divine Presence comes forth, the manifestation of the New earth will come forward, and your choice to participate in this Divine unfolding is already in motion.

May you celebrate this moment as you empower your Divine Presence with every breath.

WISDOM FROM
ARCHANGEL ZADKIEL

ARCHANGEL ZADKIEL SPEAKS:

It is with great and glorious pleasure that we are here with you! Beloved beings of a grand experience you know as LIFE! We love this word, life, because it is an uplifting word is it not? It is a great and uplifting word when you say it with great Joy... "LIFE"!

Or, you might say La Vida and you get even more excited. Indeed.

For many eons in your experience as Divine travelers of great light you have been pulsing as they say, across many dimensions, streams of light, and energy fields.

Sri and Kira discovered this beautiful oil painting of Archangel Zadkiel while in Peru. It now hangs in the TOSA Lotus Temple at TOSA Ranch, New Mexico.

When you feel a pulse of light it is similar beloved ones to the pulse of your heart. Many say; How do I know, how can I know? Help me understand.

We say, you are a pulse; you are a great pulsing beat. And you are heart beat is a great pulsing energy indeed.

When you consciously connect a great beam of Divine Illumination brought in through what you call the crown chakra of the head, and you bring that beam into your heart, and then you send it out as a great pulse beat, it connects indeed with another pulse beat even if the pulse beat it connects with has no conscious recognition of what this connection is, the experience of the connection of the heart becomes a great gift indeed. A great gift indeed.

Beloved beings, as you claim this pulsing energy of divine expanding light, and as you offer to yourself the gift of Divine Illumination, what you rediscover is the recognition that the multiple repetitive cycles of incarnation, here in a world of green and blue energy, become released with the effortless moment of breath.

Let us offer this to you with an explanation.

What we wish for you to hear, feel, see, and experience in all-ways, is for you to understand. To remember that in your experience of divine incarnations, in a world that you have come to know as earth, this has been just one cycle of your divine experience.

To allow yourself to go beyond this one cycle of experience; to let go as they say. To let go of an attachment to a single planet of experience frees the wisdom that you already carry within you to recognize all that you are without limitation.

To contain yourself within a single planetary experience is to limit the wisdom you draw upon to exist now as a being of Divine Light.

For example, in one hand you have earth: "earth" is a funny name, is it not funny when you really listen to it…earth! We enjoy Gaia. "Gaia"—feel the energy difference. Gaia is much more expansive.

Hold out your hand and call forth the energy as you say Gaia and you illuminate the hand as Gaia. Now feel Gaia transforming into a Lotus in your hand….because a Lotus beloved ones has become such a great symbol of divine awakening in a world of Gaia, because a Lotus will grow in what seems to be the muck and the mire.

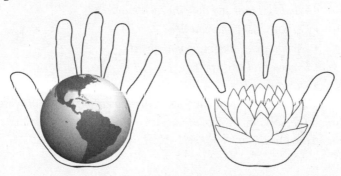

And indeed your Gaia, your beloved earth, is offering herself great growth, especially at the time of what may seem like muck and mire.

Now, with this hand out and illuminated, you bring out the other hand and you say: Show me! Show me beyond the Gaia in whatever way for me I can experience beyond the Gaia.

Some of you may already see. Some of you may already feel. Some of you may know. Some of you may say, Well perhaps I am not sure. Well then, pretend.

Allow yourself to put whatever you need to in that hand. Yes. And you notice that your hands feel different and yet they are hands of the same body.

Do you understand? Hands of the same body in a world of experience now, yet each feels different, and together they harmonize.

Now hold your hands one to the other in any way you feel called to hold them and feel your hands as a reunification energy that brings with it the opportunity to once again expand your co-creative principles without karmic ramification or imperative.

We feel this is most important to chat with you about.

Karmic imperative.

Karmic ramification.

Karmic experience.

You all know this word, karmic, yes?

This word, Karmic, is again a birth of density alignment. So many of you EssSeeNah have come to this planet, earth, to be here. You come here. You exist here. And then, do you live here?

It would be like taking out one hand and saying 'exist', and in the other hand, 'la Vida...life! Exist or la Vida...life.

• What is it that you do with each moment?
• Do you exist or do you live?
• Do you remember or do you forget?
• Do you heal or do you hurt?
• Do you say yes or do you say no?

These are the Divine energies of all momentous action of beings in form, in choices that are made with every breath. This is quite amazing! You get to breathe, hurt or heal? What was that breath?

What would you like it to be? Hurt or heal?

Because if you are hurting you are not healing, and if you are healing you are not hurting. When you breathe in, do you breathe in the energy of, I feel crummy? Then that was a hurting breath. Or, do you breathe in and say, Oh, I feel the love of the universe because I am breathing...it is a good moment.

For as you are still breathing, it is a really good moment.

Hurt or heal? What is your breath? Is your breath yes or no? Because your planet, Gaia, is asking you, is it yes or no?

If you breathe in sarcasm, doubt, guilt, anger, frustration, shoula, woulda, coulda, then you are breathing in no. And with every exhale Gaia feels you, she feels your no, and responds with OK, I will just be.

And when you breathe in 'yes', Gaia celebrates with you and another leaf is born, another flower grows, another new angel says yes to the womb of a mother who is ready to bring that angel to form.

Did you know you were that powerful?

It is your 'yes' that brings children to this world. It is your 'yes' that attracts crystalline beings of light. They are coming to your planet now with great abundant floods of energy; to be here, to witness all. You are great beings of Divine crystalline light, in full expanded EssSeeNah remembrance, if, of course, you choose to.

And you say, Zadkiel! What does all this have to do with karmic ramifications?

We say, everything beloved ones. Everything, everything!

Because in the everything, in the karmic ramification of the everything, you breathe freedom. You breathe freedom.

When your world entered this phase of divine reunification, and please remember the words that we offer you are the words of a limited world that uses vocal chords to communicate, and so we offer to you great energetic connections as we speak to you with this voice, and yet so many of you hear us beyond the voice; A great celebration indeed. Let us go back.

And so as you have entered this phase of Divine reunification, your world as they say began a great tango, a great dance indeed. A swirling and a twirling with great grace and ease, that says to all who choose to hear, who choose to breathe, who choose to be, what do you want? Because you are now the one who chooses. Good!

Your karmic imperative became a great up swell of energy upon arriving at a planet of great density with great protection: Great density with great protection.

So many of thee who arrived in full recognition of their divine service as beings of light coming into density fell fully into the forget-fulness of the expansion and aligned with the karmic energies and fell deeply into many lifetimes of alignment and belief that much more had to happen as they say.

And for many experiences, many experiences, there was a procession of experience and the procession of experience is a great wellspring of knowledge. There is the process of experience in your world. Some places call this many things, but there is the procession of experience, it does not have an order, so do not try to order it.

The procession of experience simply says, I will reincarnate, rein-carnate, reincarnate, reincarnate, again and again and again until the moment of divine reunification under the auspicious of karmic impera-tive and ramification. Thereby expanding the light filled experience with each incarnation.

This is a beautiful imperative indeed, during a time of energetic recognition and the calling forth of great energies to your world.

And so, let us skip ahead now, to what you call the millennium, and then we will skip ahead to two other dates in your world. One you call 2012 and the other you call 2020.

The date of the millennium, was the first stage of a great expansion of energy that ushered in the time of reunification and lifted the karmic imperative of your world. In this great time of the post impetus of the divine reconnection, many are afraid.

*When many are afraid they become resistant and
concerned, because in their fear, they recognize that they are
responsible in their way of expression.*

*To be fully awake to your responsible expression of light expanding
can be quite fearful as there is no one to blame. Goodness gracious, in
a world of blame that can be very scary and lonely.*

*In a world that is blame-less there is only enlightenment.
In a world that is not enlightened, there is only blame.*

*And so beloved ones, to find thyself in the enlightened phase
is simply to align with the light in your divine field of energy
without blame.*

*In your world now, so popular, past life do this do that, indeed,
it is but a moment to reflect upon, to smile at, and to embrace without
blame. To live in the past, is to negate the now and to eliminate the
future. In a world that lives in the past, the past will repeat itself and
in your world now, the past is getting ready to repeat itself as a world.*

How do you wish to be in that beloved ones?

*There are two dates upon you that in what you call linear time,
and we often will do our best to not discuss linear time, in a moment,
right now, we will discuss the 2012 with you.*

*What we wish to share with you is this, when the past repeats itself,
you have a choice, you have a choice to participate with the energy of
your own past, or you have the choice to bring forward the energy of
momentum of the future.*

*When you bring your attention to the past, you ignite the past.
When you bring your heart to the presence of now, you ignite
now. When you are able to ignite yourself without the karmic
imperative propelling you; you open up a corridor of divine
co-creative freedom that will shift all negativity.*

If you choose it to. You begin with yourself. If you try to save the world you will usually get very tired. Ignite yourself.

Many cross their arms and say we must save the world. OK, but take a lot of vitamins, you will be tired!

And as you do, and as you ignite and as you reignite yourself and claim yourself and free yourself you will free your world and you will "Save" your world.

Because your world is in your hands, is it not?

Lift up that hand again that had Gaia, feel that lotus growing now, what does it feel like now? And lift up your other hand and see 2020 in your hand, what does it feel like now and what would you like it to feel like?

Bring your hands together and feel this energy ignite. Because each time you bring your hands together and you feel this energy ignite you are offering a blessing to this world, you are offering ignition and fuel, for a greater future not a repeat of one you have done many times.

Where is your heart now and where do you wish it to be?

In your world, beloved ones, we are all here. We are dancing often. Do you dance often? Do! Even if you must close your door so no one see, it is OK…dance often. And if you say you cannot dance, then close your eyes and see yourself dancing. Dance often.

Feel yourself like a butterfly move your arms like wings and dance often and giggle. Because when you giggle and dance often, you are sending out great wave and energies to a planet that is asking, Is anyone dancing anymore? With love?

Because reverence and love are the gifts of divine presence. Reverence and love are the gifts of divine presence. And reverence, beloved ones, is not about being in a house designated as holy. The designated holy house is with you right now. You are the designated holy house. In your world they say where two or more are gathered…you have two hands. Gather them and be in your holy house.

You are the holy house, you are the reverence you are the greatest gift that has ever been and Gaia is the greatest gift you have ever co-created. And you are not done.

Yet, you are pretty cooked. It is a banquet is it not, and you are ready.

Seek yourself.
Seek your truth.
From this your world will expand evermore.

QUESTION FROM THE AUDIENCE: What can we do to assist the anchoring of our soul in our heart as we move through this time of change?

This is a beautiful question.

To invite the anchoring of the heart to even ask the question is a celebration. Dance in little circles, drink fermented grape and say 'whoo-hoo'! Because when one invites the anchoring of the heart, one is inviting the upliftment of the Self, thereby co-creating the upliftment of the all into the one.

When you ask what can one do to anchor this gift, we offer to you first, in all funny seriousness, the dancing, the smiling, the twirling, when the physical body twirls you move fields of energy that seek to attach and lower the fields frequency of holding heart energy.

Often begin by taking one had to the lower spine point of the body, or what many call the root center, and the next hand to the second chakra, then the other hand to the third chakra, and after you have breathed to these chakras bring your hands straight out to the sides, and then pick one hand, it does not matter which one, and you stare at it, you take in a deep breath, you exhale and you spin. And you spin.

And if you get dizzy, do not worry, keep going, spin slower.

And when you are done, so many say, how many times, spin until you wish to stop and then you bring your hands to your heart and you take a deep breath and you feel those three chakras of the lower body...stable.

And you feel your heart expand, and then you feel Raphael, Michael, Zadkiel, and a fourth that will come as you invite to form a diamond around you, and as we form this diamond around you, you will feel gold and green energy interweaving at your heart center, and will feel suddenly and notice that you are not longer standing on the ground, that it is now an inch or so below you and you will understand the gift of being lifted and supported.

Do this often beloved one and smile more and dance more and sing more and remember who you are. All of this will integrate together.

QUESTION FROM THE AUDIENCE: What do we need to know?

This is a very important question, because in your world now there is a great cry for the need to know. Need to know about a date, need to know about an energy or experience, need to know about the future, need to know about everything, indeed.

The power of need to know limits the expansion of truth. The ability to understand through the gift of divine presence expands the truth.

Bring your hand to your heart center often. Breathe in all questions and let go of the need to know and to recognize all that you do know. To trust that which comes forward through the recognition that all great wisdom reveals itself in the perfect moment and with perfect timing and with perfect harmony and synergy with all that has ever been.

You do know and you understand when you breathe into that peace and all is revealed with great presence and wondrous momentum and miraculous unfoldment that your mind says, can not keep up…nor should it have to. It needs a rest, so send it on vacation. Yes, indeed.

Beloved beings of Gaia, your world is asking you what you want to do. Allow your clarity to come from your heart. And if you ask, How do I do that, dear goodness how do I do that my mind is so strong, then you take a deep breath and in that one breath you can say yes or you can say no.

You can hurt or you can heal, you can be whole or you can be less than whole. What do you want? What do you want for your world?

We love you beloved beings and we are here for you all-ways!

We are grateful that you are here. With each breath may you remember that this is the moment you came for. What are you dong with it? It is your choice.

We love you dearly.
Feel our love around you.
Feel our hearts around you.
Beloved ones, you are not ever alone.
When you cry out we are already there.
When you scream out we are already there.
When your mind tries to tell you we are not there, we are there.
When you doubt, when you kick, when you cry,
we are there, as you are here.
We love you.
And so it is!

ENDNOTES

This list represents the endnotes that are referenced throughout the book. Rather than format by chapter, they have simply been enumerated sequentially for ease of location.

1   *Lost Books of the Essene*: A series of energy transmissions through Sri Ram Kaa and Kira Raa that consists of twelve lessons. You can learn more and find all the lessons at www.SriandKira.com.

2   *The Lost Books of the Essene, Book Seven: Reverent Upliftment.*

3   *The Divine Illuminations: Lesson One.* This is a series of timeless EssSeeNah (Essene) revelations through Sri Ram Kaa and Kira Raa. You can learn more and find all the lessons at www.Sriand Kira.com.

4   This is the process of Archangelic In-soulment, whereby Kira Raa is able to completely leave her body and allow for the archangelic realm to speak through her without any egoic filter or personality presence. This story is revealed in its entirety in the book *Sacred Union: The Journey Home.*

5   It is a very rare gift for the high priest and his wife, a healing shaman, to work with non-indigenous people. They, along with several others, have come forward in recognition of the unification of the eagle and the condor to work with all visitors to TOSA La Laguna as part of the reunification of these times.

6   Angelic Oracle Kira Raa first died of cancer on the operating table in 1989 during surgery. Clinically pronounced dead, her journey during her death and conscious decision to return to the planet re-ignited her childhood psychic abilities and prepared her to move forward with the process of Archangelic In-soulment.

7   This is a direct quote from Archangel Zadkiel.

8   Because of its near perfect year-round weather, Guatemala is often referred to as the Land of Eternal Spring.

9   The Golden Ray program is an advanced energetic training that is offered to all students after they have completed the home study course, Navigating the Inner Matrix.

10 The rich Mayan native languages of the Cakchiquel and the Quiché are extraordinarily creative and call forth great symbol-

ism. They are unique in their expression and each dialect is filled with rich heritage. There are many Mayan languages still alive within Guatemala, and the highland Maya of the lake region predominately speak either Cakchiquel or Quiché.

11 Referring to Dorothy from *The Wizard of Oz* as she first stepped out of her house into Munchkin land and the film shifts from black-and-white to color.

12 It is important to note here in the era of ceremonies that are often done using some form of hallucinogenic herb, we were fully present and drug free. The path of Self-Ascension and the direct connection with archangelic realms is so profoundly life altering that any form of artificial stimulant pales in the energy of pure mystical experience. Indeed, it will diminish it.

13 The TOSA Miracle Team is a group of committed individuals who have come together to hold presence, love and miracle manifestation energy for the planet. Many remember being team members in past lives, and have always known there was a greater sense of community waiting for them now. To learn more about the TOSA Miracle Team, please visit www.SriandKira.com.

14 The Benevolent Ones are divine crystalline beings from the 33rd dimension that have not ever taken form on our planet before. They are here as guardians, or custodians of those light workers who seek to awaken.

15 From the *Divine Illuminations Series, Lesson Two*.

16 Kaminal Juyú, located in the western area of Guatemala City, is one of the most important sites of the pre-Hispanic period. While its history dates back to the Early Pre-classical Period, the actual inhabitants of this ancient city are yet unknown, since remains have disclosed the presence of various cultural groups.

17 The Essene Brethren have come forward at this moment on our planet to once again offer great healing through the awakened presence of humanity. Ess-See-Nah is the energy of these beings, and as you breathe the word *Ess-See-Nah* you discover greater spaciousness within their messages. *The Lost Books of the Essene* is a series of twelve books delivered through Angelic Oracle Kira Raa.

18 The Ascended Master Jeshua is most commonly referred to as Jesus or Jesus Christ.

19 This is from the *Divine Illuiminations series, Lesson One*.

20 This is from the *Divine Illuminations, Book Two*.

21 Soul Nourishment is a system of nourishing and sustaining the body through light-filled energy and foods that was gifted to the planet through the Archangelic realm. This system was first revealed in the book *Sacred Union: The Journey Home*.

22 The "T-12" is a name offered by a group of ascended beings who have stepped forward to offer guidance to humanity at the cycles of the ages. When Sri asked "Who is talking?" they replied with laughter, "We are a collective of 12 energies. You could call us the Tribe of 12, or just T-12."

23 Su'laria is the original Atlantis, and it did not exist on this planet. It was the cosmic predecessor that birthed the Atlantis on planet earth. This cosmology and history is fully explained in the book *2012: Atlantean Revelations*.

24 This is from the *Divine Illuminations, Book Two*.

25 This is a direct quote from Archangel Zadkiel.

26 Early in 2007, Sri and Kira received a powerful message from the Ascended Master St. Germaine to arrive at the headwaters of the Ganges on December 17, 2008, to open the Dome of Divine Protection. This became quite an important revelation, as they arrived just days after the Mumbai terrorist attack and as Pakistan was once again becoming a hotbed of possible world-threatening activity. Despite the world cry to not enter the country, Sri, Kira and 21 brave souls arrived at the headwaters as directed and were greeted by hundreds of Sadus on the banks of the river, who simply "knew" they were coming.

27 A direct quote from Mahatma Gandhi.

28 The practices of Self-Ascension are numerous and simple to apply to your life. You can find many of these practices in any of the books written by Sri and Kira and also posted free at the website www.SriandKira.com.

29 The Bible, Luke 17:20–21.

30   In 1989, Kira Raa died on the operating table from cancer. During this transition experience she was declared clinically dead while her soul as experiencing great choices and illuminations prior to returning to her body.

31   The word *priests* is used to generically infer any clergy of a dogmatic religious belief system.

32   This powerful lesson is one of the lessons of light. You can read more about these lessons in the book *2012: Atlantean Revelations*.

33   In our very first dialogues with Archangel Zadkiel, he refers to us as travelers. This is fully shared in the book *Sacred Union: The Journey Home*.

34   These are references to public appearances and workshops given by Sri and Kira.

35   From the *Divine Illuminations Series, Lesson Three: The Moment of Balance*.

36   Several documented studies demonstrate that meditation calms dysfunctional behavior. For example, see Dillbeck M. C., et al. The Transcendental Meditation program and crime rate reduction in a sample of forty-eight cities. *Journal of Crime and Justice* 4:25–45, 1981.

ABOUT THE AUTHORS

Sri Ram Kaa and **Kira Raa** are the founders of the Avesa Quantum Healing Institute, the TOSA Center for Enlightened Living in New Mexico and the TOSA La Laguna Self-Ascension Center at Lake Atitlán, Guatemala. Wisdom Teacher Sri Ram Kaa is a gifted psychotherapist, skilled medical intuitive and Master Avesa Quantum Healer. Angelic Oracle Kira Raa has been clairvoyant since childhood and was declared clinically dead of cancer in 1989. She is now widely accepted as the most profound Archangelic Oracle of our time and is also a Master Avesa Quantum Healer. Together they have appeared on numerous TV shows and are monthly columnists for *Awareness* magazine and *UFO* magazine. Find Sri and Kira online at www.Sri andKira.com and learn more at www.SelfAscension.com. They live in Tijeres, New Mexico.